lonely planet

ICELAND'S
RING ROAD

- - - - - - - - - - - - - - - -

ROAD
TRIPS

Alexis Averbuck, Carolyn Bain,
Jade Bremner, Belinda Dixon

HOW TO USE THIS BOOK

Reviews

In the Destinations section:

All reviews are ordered in our authors' preference, starting with their most preferred option. Additionally:

Sights are arranged in the geographic order that we suggest you visit them and, within this order, by author preference.

Eating and Sleeping reviews are ordered by price range (budget, midrange, top end) and, within these ranges, by author preference.

Map Legend

Routes
- Trip Route
- Trip Detour
- Linked Trip
- Walk Route
- Tollway
- Freeway
- Primary
- Secondary
- Tertiary
- Lane
- Unsealed Road
- Plaza/Mall
- Steps
- Tunnel
- Pedestrian Overpass
- Walk Track/Path

Boundaries
- International
- State/Province
- Cliff

Hydrography
- River/Creek
- Intermittent River
- Swamp/Mangrove
- Canal
- Water
- Dry/Salt/ Intermittent Lake
- Glacier

Highway Markers
- A20 Highway marker

Trips
- 1 Trip Numbers
- 9 Trip Stop
- Walking tour
- Trip Detour

Population
- ✪ Capital (National)
- ◉ Capital (State/Province)
- ● City/Large Town
- ● Town/Village

Areas
- Beach
- Glacier
- Cemetery (Christian)
- Cemetery (Other)
- Park
- Forest
- Reservation
- Urban Area
- Sportsground

Transport
- ✈ Airport
- Cable Car/ Funicular
- Ⓜ Metro station
- Ⓟ Parking
- Train/Railway
- Tram

Note: Not all symbols displayed above appear on the maps in this book

Symbols In This Book

- ✓ Top Tips
- S Link Your Trips
- Q Tips from Locals
- Trip Detour
- History & Culture
- Family

- Food & Drink
- Outdoors
- Essential Photo
- Walking Tour
- Eating
- Sleeping

- ◉ Sights
- Beaches
- Activities
- Courses
- Tours
- Festivals & Events

- Sleeping
- Eating
- Drinking
- Entertainment
- Shopping
- Information & Transport

These symbols and abbreviations give vital information for each listing:

- ☎ Telephone number
- ⏰ Opening hours
- P Parking
- ⊖ Nonsmoking
- ❄ Air-conditioning
- @ Internet access
- 🛜 Wi-fi access
- ≋ Swimming pool
- 🥗 Vegetarian selection
- 📖 English-language menu
- 👪 Family-friendly

- 🐾 Pet-friendly
- 🚌 Bus
- ⛴ Ferry
- 🚊 Tram
- 🚆 Train
- apt apartments
- d double rooms
- dm dorm beds
- q quad rooms
- r rooms
- s single rooms
- ste suites
- tr triple rooms
- tw twin rooms

CONTENTS

PLAN YOUR TRIP

ROAD TRIPS

DESTINATIONS

ROAD TRIP ESSENTIALS.... 106

COVID-19

We have re-checked every business in this book before publication to ensure that it is still open after 2020's COVID-19 outbreak. However, the economic and social impacts of COVID-19 will continue to be felt long after the outbreak has been contained, and many businesses, services and events referenced in this guide may experience ongoing restrictions. Some businesses may be temporarily closed, have changed their opening hours and services, or require bookings; some unfortunately could have closed permanently. We suggest you check with venues before visiting for the latest information.

WELCOME TO
ICELAND'S
RING ROAD

Hitting headlines, topping bucket lists, wooing nature lovers and dazzling increasing numbers of visitors: Iceland, an underpopulated island marooned near the top of the globe, is literally a country in the making. It's a vast volcanic laboratory where mighty forces shape the earth: geysers gush, mudpots gloop, ice-covered volcanoes rumble and glaciers cut great pathways through the mountains. Its supercharged splendour seems designed to remind visitors of their utter insignificance in the greater scheme of things.

Bravely forging through the geological magnificence is the Ring Road, Iceland's Route 1, which joins nearly all the places you can get to without a serious 4WD in one long circumnavigation of the island. Epic doesn't even begin to describe this road trip, but it's not only about jaw-dropping vistas: the counterpoint to so much natural beauty is found in Iceland's vibrant cultural life, handicrafts and locavore cuisine, and the warmth of its creative, no-nonsense, welcoming people. It's a drive like no other.

The Ring Road between Jökulsárlón (p37) and Höfn (p39)

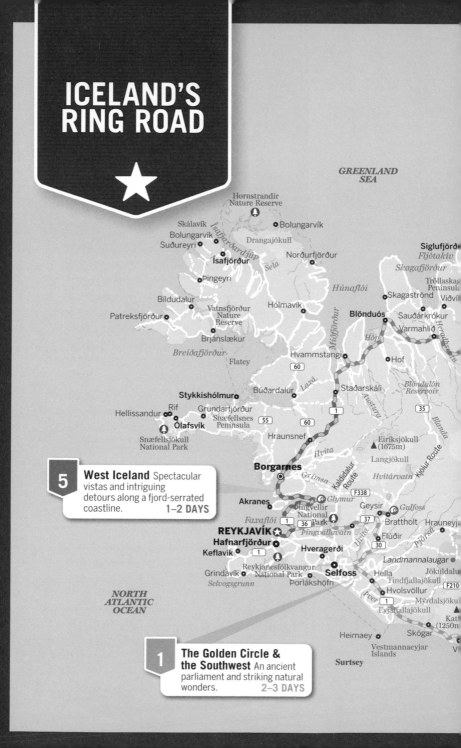

ICELAND'S RING ROAD

GREENLAND SEA

Hornstrandir
Nature Reserve

Skálavík
Bolungarvík
Suðureyri

Bolungarvík

Drangajökull

Ísafjörður

Norðurfjörður

Ísafjarðardjúp

Sela

Siglufjörð
Fljótakív

Skagafjörður

Þingeyri

Tröllaskac
Peninsula

Húnaflói

Skagaströnd   Viðvi

Bíldudalur

Hólmavík

Vatnsfjörður
Nature
Reserve

Blönduós

Sauðárkrókur

Patreksfjörður

Varmahlíð

Brjánslækur

Hóp

Hvammstangi

Hof

Breiðafjörður   Flatey

60

*Blöndulón
Reservoir*

Búðardalur

Staðarskáli

Austura

Stykkishólmur

Laxá

35

Hellissandur   Rif   Grundarfjörður
Ólafsvík   Snæfellsnes
Peninsula

55   60

Staðarskáli

1

Blanda

Eiríksjökull
▲(1675m)

Snæfellsjökull
National Park

Hraunsnef

Hvítá

Langjökull

Hvítárvatn

Kjölur Route

Borgarnes

Grímsa

Kaldidalur
Route

F338

---

5 **West Iceland** Spectacular
vistas and intriguing
detours along a fjord-serrated
coastline. **1–2 DAYS**

Akranes

Glymur

Geysir   *Gulfoss*

Þingvellir
National
Park

37

Bratholt   Hrauneyja

REYKJAVÍK ✪

Faxaflói

36   Þingvallavatn

Flúðir

Þjórsá

Hafnarfjörður

Hvítá

30

Keflavík   1

Landmannalaugar

Grindavík   Reykjanesfólkvangur
National Park

Hveragerði

Hella   Jökuldalu

**NORTH
ATLANTIC
OCEAN**

Selvogsgrunn   Þorlákshöfn

Selfoss

Tindfjallajökull   F210

Hvolsvöllur

Mýrdalsjökul

1

Eyjafjallajökull   ▲

Þverá

Kat
(1250n

Heimaey

Skógar

Vestmannaeyjar
Islands

Ví

Surtsey

---

1 **The Golden Circle &
the Southwest** An ancient
parliament and striking natural
wonders. **2–3 DAYS**

3 **North Iceland**
Iceland's geological indigestion is obvious in belching mud and stark lava fields. **4–5 DAYS**

GREENLAND SEA

Grímsey

870

Flatey
Öxarfjörður
Þistilfjörður
85
Djúpa
Bakkaflói
Jökulsárgljúfur (Vatnajökull National Park – North)
ðlafsfjörður   Húsavík
í Fjörðum   87
Sanda   *Kverfa*
olvík   ○Bakkafjörður
Sela
○Dettifoss
○Vopnafjörður
Akureyri   1
Goðafoss   Reykjahlíð   85   *Hofsá*
rkjökull   Skútustaðir   *Mývatn*   ○Njarðvík
Hörgá   *Jökulsá á Fjöllum*
Aldeyjarfoss   ○Húsavík
F26   1   Egilsstaðir   **Seyðisfjörður**
Hengifossárvatn   92   Neskaupstaðir
Fnjóská   Reyðarfjörður ○Eskifjörður
Askja   *Hálslón Reservoir*   Fáskrúðsfjörður
Sprengisandur Route   *Kverkfjöll Route*   *Jökulsá*
Dyngjujökull   Öxi Pass   ○Stöðvarfjörður
Kverká   Breiðdalsvík
▲Bárðarbunga (2009m)   *Þrándarjökull*   ○Djúpivogur
fsjökull   Kverkfjöll (1860m)   *Eyjabakkajökull*
F26   Grímsvötn (1719m)   Vatnajökull   Hoffellsjökull   Stafafell
Hágöngulón   Fláajökull   *Lón*
rísvatn   Heinabergsjökull   Bjarnanes   *Lónsvík*
Kaldakvísl   Skaftafell (Vatnajökull National Park – South)   ○Stokksnes
Tungnaá   Siðujökull   **Höfn**
Laki Route   Hvannadalshnúkur (2110m)   Breiðamerkurjökull
rkjufell   Skaftafell   ○Öræfajökull
Skaftá   Hof
Núpsá   1
1   Kirkjubæjarklaustur
Hólmsá
Kúðafljót

3 **East Iceland**
Capering puffins and black sand beaches characterise this less-visited region. **2–3 DAYS**

NORTH ATLANTIC OCEAN

2 **Southeast Iceland**
Majestic glaciers calve seabound icebergs on this awe-inspiring stretch. **3–4 DAYS**

(N) 0 ▬▬▬▬▬▬ 100 km
0 ▬▬▬▬▬▬ 50 miles

ICELAND'S RING ROAD
HIGHLIGHTS
★

Jökulsárlón A ghostly procession of luminous blue icebergs drifts serenely through the 25-sq-km Jökulsárlón lagoon before floating out to sea. See it on Trip **2**

Skaftafell A gem in the expansive Vatnajökull National Park, Skaftafell encompasses a spellbinding wilderness of glaciers, volcanoes and mountains. See it on Trip **2**

Reykjavík A vibrant cultural hub, the capital boasts music, museums, shopping, interesting architecture and a staggering number of coffeehouses serving designer microbrews. See it on Trip **5**

CITY GUIDE

REYKJAVÍK

Although tiny in size, Reykjavík has a huge cultural presence. Imaginative Reykjavikers embrace their sense of community and bring a joy to life, creating captivating museums, cool music, and offbeat cafes and bars. The city is also a superb base for touring Iceland's natural wonders: glacier-topped volcanoes, shimmering falls and black-sand beaches.

Reykjavíc The view from Hallgrímskirkja (p72)

Getting Around

You won't really need the car in Reykjavík itself. Walking is the best way to see the compact centre, while there's excellent bus coverage around the town.

Parking

Street parking in the city centre is limited and costs 320kr per hour in the Red Zone and 170kr per hour in the Blue, Green and Yellow Zones. You must pay between 9am and 6pm from Monday to Friday and from 10am to 4pm Saturday.

Where to Eat

Little Reykjavík has an astonishing assortment of eateries. Loads of seafood and Icelandic or New Nordic restaurants serve tried-and-true variations on local fish and lamb, but the capital is also the main spot for finding international eats.

Where to Stay

Reykjavík has loads of accommodation choices, with hostels, midrange guesthouses (often with shared bathrooms and kitchen) and business-class hotels galore, and top-end boutique hotels and apartments seem to be opening daily. June through August accommodation books out entirely; reservations are essential.

Useful Websites

Visit Reykjavík (www.visitreykjavik.is) Official site.

Reykjavík Grapevine (www.grapevine.is) Great English-language newspaper and website.

Lonely Planet (www.lonelyplanet.com/iceland/reykjavic) Destination information and more.

TOP EXPERIENCES

➜ **Old Reykjavík**
Explore this historic quarter and shopping in nearby Laugavegur and the capital's many design boutiques.

➜ **National Museum**
Learn about Iceland's settlement and fascinating history.

➜ **Old Harbour Dining**
The Old Harbour is loaded with excellent eating options.

➜ **Hallgrímskirkja**
Photograph the striking exterior then zip up for sweeping views from this landmark's modernist steeple.

➜ **Whale Watching**
Sight the whales leaping off Iceland's shores on an excursion from the Old Harbour.

➜ **Reykjavík Art Museum**
Check out contemporary art from installations to paintings and sculpture at the three branches of this well-curated art magnet.

➜ **Settlement Exhibition**
Peruse a Viking longhouse and artefacts from Reykjavík's first days.

➜ **Harpa**
Enjoy a performance or simply be dazzled by the shiny surfaces and gorgeous interior of Reykjavík's iconic concert hall.

➜ **Cafes**
Sidle up to cool cats sipping coffee at quirky cafes.

➜ **Laugardalur**
Soak at the geothermal pool or stroll through botanical gardens.

➜ **Culture House**
Examine a mix of art, artefacts and manuscripts illustrating Iceland's interesting history.

NEED TO KNOW

CURRENCY
Icelandic króna (kr or ISK)

LANGUAGE
Icelandic; English widely spoken

VISAS
Generally not required for stays of up to 90 days.

FUEL
Petrol stations are regularly spaced but check the distance to the next station when in the highlands. At research time, fuel cost about kr225/L.

RENTAL CARS
Some of the numerous car-hire companies:

Átak (www.atak.is)

Europcar (www.europcar.is)

Geysir (www.geysir.is)

SADcars (www.sadcars.com)

IMPORTANT NUMBERS
Make sure you get a breakdown number from your rental provider.

Emergency Services (📞112)

Weather forecast (📞902 0600, press 1 after the introduction)

Road condition information (📞1777)

Climate

Mild summers, cold winters

Ísafjörður
GO May–Sep

Akureyri
GO year-round

Egilsstaðir
GO May–Sep

Reykjavík
GO year-round

Þórsmörk
GO May–Sep

When to Go

High Season (Jun–Aug)
» Visitors descend en masse, especially to Reykjavík and the south. Prices peak; prebookings are essential.

» Endless daylight, plentiful festivals, busy activities.

» Highland mountain roads open to 4WDs from mid-June or later; hikers welcome.

Shoulder (May & Sep)
» Breezier weather; occasional snows in the highlands (access via mountain roads is weather-dependent).

» Optimal visiting conditions if you prefer smaller crowds and lower prices over cloudless days.

Low Season (Oct–Apr)
» Mountain roads closed; some minor roads shut due to weather conditions.

» Winter activities on offer, including skiing, snowshoeing and visiting ice caves.

» Brief spurts of daylight; long nights with possible Northern Lights viewings.

» New Year's Eve in Reykjavík is becoming a big tourist event.

Daily Costs

Budget: Less than 18,000kr

» Camping: 1500–1800kr

» Dorm bed: 4000–7000kr

» Hostel breakfast: 1800–2000kr

» Grill-bar meal or soup lunch: 1500–2200kr

Midrange: 18,000–35,000kr

» Guesthouse double room: 18,000–28,000kr

» Cafe meal: 2000–3500kr

» Museum entry: 1000kr

» Small vehicle rental (per day): from 8000kr

Top end: More than 35,000kr

» Boutique double room: 30,000–45,000kr

» Main dish in top-end restaurant: 3500–7000kr

» 4WD rental (per day): from 15,000kr

Eating

Restaurants Across the country, the emphasis is on farm-fresh, local produce.

Cafes Open usually from lunchtime into evening, serving simple fare.

Accommodation In rural areas, guesthouses and hotels may offer meals.

Grill bars Often found at petrol stations. Standby for hot dogs and burgers, plus simple soup, fish and lamb dishes.

Vegetarians No problem in Reykjavík. Elsewhere, usually there's at least one veggie item on menus, but it's often boring.

Sleeping

Hotels From small, bland and businesslike to designer dens with all the trimmings.

Guesthouses Run the gamut from homestyle B&Bs to large hotel-like properties.

Hostels Popular budget options, spread across the country.

Campgrounds No requirement to book. Exposure to the elements. Campervans increasingly popular.

Arriving in Iceland

Keflavík International Airport

Bus Public buses (kr1680) and door-to-door shuttle bus companies (kr2100 to 2700) run the 48km into Reykjavík.

Car Can be rented from the airport; prebook.

Taxis Not heavily utilised due to efficient buses and high cost (kr15,000).

Mobile Phones

Mobile (cell) coverage is widespread. Visitors with GSM phones can make roaming calls; purchase a local SIM card if you're staying a while.

Internet Access

Wi-fi is available in most accommodation and eating venues across the country, as well as in service stations. The easiest way to get online is to purchase a local SIM card with data package.

Money

Iceland is virtually cashless: cards reign supreme, even in the most rural reaches. ATMs available in all towns. As service and VAT taxes are always included in prices, tipping isn't required. At restaurants, rounding up the bill or leaving a small tip for good service is appreciated.

Useful Websites

Icelandic Met Office (http://en.vedur.is) Best resource for weather forecasts.

Icelandic Road Administration (www.road.is) Details road openings and current conditions.

Lonely Planet (www.lonelyplanet.com/iceland) Destination information, hotel bookings, traveller forum and more.

Safe Travel (www.safetravel.is) Stay safe while travelling.

Visit Iceland (www.visiticeland.com) Iceland's official tourism portal.

Opening Hours

Opening hours vary throughout the year (some places are closed outside the high season). In general hours tend to be longer from June to August, and shorter from September to May. See p117 for standard opening hours.

> For more, see Iceland Driving Guide (p112).

Ring Road Planner

Unless you've visited Iceland before, you'll likely struggle to name an Icelandic town besides Reykjavík. You may worry about planning your visit when so much of the country is vast and unknown. Fear not, the path is clear: take the Ring Road.

Best Ring Road Detours

Snæfellsnes Peninsula

A veritable ring road unto itself that takes in lava fields, wild coastline and an infamous ice cap; 200km detour.

Tröllaskagi Peninsula

Follow Rte 76/Rte 82 as it climbs up towards the Arctic – hair-raising road tunnels and scenic panoramas await; 90km detour.

Borgarfjörður Eystri

Take Rte 94 through rhyolite cliffs and down into this quiet hamlet where there are visiting puffins and superb hiking trails; 150km detour.

Vestmannaeyjar

Hop on the ferry at Landeyjahöfn to discover a rugged archipelago of islets; 30km detour plus a 30-minute boat ride each way.

Þórsmörk

Park at Seljalandsfoss and take the bus into a forested kingdom rife with scenic walks; 50km detour along a rutty road accessible only by certified vehicles; hiking also an option.

The 'Diamond Circle'

Dreamed up by marketers, the Diamond Circle barrels north from Mývatn to take in the whale-filled bay of Húsavík, the grand canyon and trails of Ásbyrgi, and the roaring falls at Dettifoss; 180km detour.

Route 1

Route 1 (Þjóðvegur 1), known as the Ring Road, is the country's main thoroughfare, comprising a super-scenic 1340km (832 miles) of paved highway. It's rarely more than one lane in either direction. Countless gems line its path, while secondary roads lead off it to further-flung adventures.

When to Go

The Ring Road is generally accessible year-round (there may be exceptions during winter storms); many of the secondary roads are closed during the colder months. Check out www.road.is for details of road closures, and www.vedur.is for weather forecasts.

Clockwise or Anticlockwise?

It doesn't matter which way you tackle the Ring Road – the landscape reveals itself in an equally cinematic fashion from both directions.

If you're travelling during the latter part of summer (August into September), we recommend driving the loop in a clockwise manner – check off your northern must-sees first as warmer weather sticks around a tad longer in the south.

How Long Do I Need?

Driving the Ring Road without stopping (or breaking the speed limit) would take approximately 16 hours. Thus, a week-long trip around the countryside means an average of about 2½ hours of driving per day. While this might seem a bit full-on for some, remember that the drive is extraordinarily scenic and rarely feels like a haul. In summer there's plenty of daylight.

A minimum of 10 days is recommended to do justice to the Ring Road (two weeks is better). For travellers planning an itinerary that's less than a week, it's better to commit to one or two regions in detail (eg Reykjavík and the south or west; or a week in the north), rather than trying to hoof it around the island.

By Car

Discovering Iceland by private vehicle is by far the most convenient way to go. It is, as you may have expected, also the most expensive option.

Renting a Car

It's best to start planning early if searching for low rates. The internet is your best resource, but take care to double-check that all fees are included in the quoted price.

Book early for summer hires – companies sometimes run out of vehicles.

2WD or 4WD?

A 2WD vehicle is fine in summer if you're planning to drive just the Ring Road and major secondary roads. If you want to explore the interior (driving on 'F' mountain roads), you'll need a more robust 4WD; alternatively, hire a 2WD and book bus trips or super-Jeep tours to less accessible areas.

In winter, 2WDs aren't recommended; consider a 4WD for safety (note, rental prices are considerably lower than in summer). Winter tyres are fitted to winter rentals.

Breaking Up the Journey

The most important thing to remember when travelling the Ring Road is to use it as a conduit to explore memorable detours. Choosing five mini-bases along the journey to break up the drive is recommended. Try selecting one stop in each region through which the Ring Road passes: the west, north, east, southeast and southwest. De-

> **RING ROAD TIPS**
> ....
> ➡ Don't confuse the Ring Road, which loops the country, with the Golden Circle (a tourist route in the country's southwest).
>
> ➡ The Ring Road doesn't traverse Iceland's interior – if you're keen to see more, two highland routes cut through the centre. These roads are only open in summer, and only to 4WDs and all-terrain buses.

pending on the length of your trip, you can spend several nights at each base, engaging in the area's best activities and detours.

By Bus

Far less convenient than car rental, Iceland's limited bus service is the most cost-effective option for solo travellers – however, in summer 2018 a reduction in services in the east meant it became very hard (but not altogether impossible) to travel the entire Ring Road by bus.

You should budget double the time of a private vehicle to loop around. For comparison, two travellers bussing around the island roughly equals the price (excluding petrol) of a small rental car for a week.

By Bicycle

Unfortunately cyclists will have a tougher time than expected travelling the Ring Road. The changeable weather makes for tough going, and although the path is paved, there is hardly any room on the shoulder of the road to provide a comfortable distance from vehicular traffic.

By Hitching & Ride-Sharing

The most cost-effective way to venture around the Ring Road is to stick out your thumb. In summer it's quite easy to hitch all the way around the Ring Road but be aware of the potential risks involved.

Many hostels have ride-share poster boards in their lobbies. A great resource is www.samferda.is, an online ride-share messageboard.

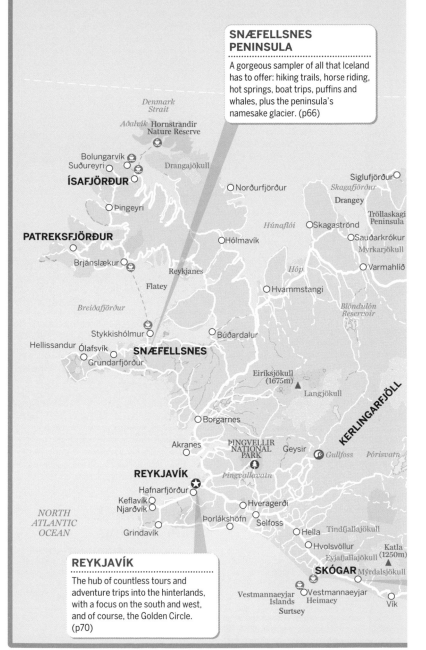

SNÆFELLSNES PENINSULA

A gorgeous sampler of all that Iceland has to offer: hiking trails, horse riding, hot springs, boat trips, puffins and whales, plus the peninsula's namesake glacier. (p66)

REYKJAVÍK

The hub of countless tours and adventure trips into the hinterlands, with a focus on the south and west, and of course, the Golden Circle. (p70)

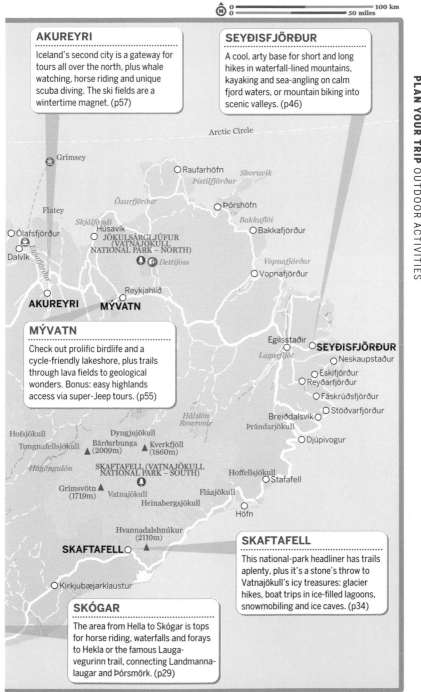

0 ——————— 100 km
0 ——————— 50 miles

AKUREYRI

Iceland's second city is a gateway for tours all over the north, plus whale watching, horse riding and unique scuba diving. The ski fields are a wintertime magnet. (p57)

SEYÐISFJÖRÐUR

A cool, arty base for short and long hikes in waterfall-lined mountains, kayaking and sea-angling on calm fjord waters, or mountain biking into scenic valleys. (p46)

Arctic Circle

Grímsey

○ Raufarhöfn   Skoruvík
Þistilfjörður

Öxarfjörður   ○ Þórshöfn

Flatey   Bakkaflói

Skjálfandi   Húsavík
○ Ólafsfjörður   ○ JÖKULSÁRGLJÚFUR   ○ Bakkafjörður
○   (VATNAJÖKULL
Dalvík   NATIONAL PARK – NORTH)
              ⊙ ⦿ Dettifoss   Vopnafjörður
                                      ○ Vopnafjörður
          Reykjahlíð
○
AKUREYRI   MÝVATN

MÝVATN

Check out prolific birdlife and a cycle-friendly lakeshore, plus trails through lava fields to geological wonders. Bonus: easy highlands access via super-Jeep tours. (p55)

Egilsstaðir
○   ○**SEYÐISFJÖRÐUR**
Lagarfljót   ○ Neskaupstaður

○ Eskifjörður
○ Reyðarfjörður
○ Fáskrúðsfjörður
○ Stöðvarfjörður
Hálslón   Breiðdalsvík ○
Reservoir   Þrándarjökull

Hofsjökull   Dyngjujökull   ○ Djúpivogur
Tungnafellsjökull   Bárðarbunga ▲ Kverkfjöll
▲(2009m)   (1860m)
Hágöngulón   SKAFTAFELL (VATNAJÖKULL
              NATIONAL PARK – SOUTH)   Hoffellsjökull
              ⊙   ○ Stafafell
Grímsvötn ▲   Fláajökull
(1719m)   Vatnajökull
          Heinabergsjökull   ○
                                Höfn

Hvannadalshnúkur
(2110m)   ## SKAFTAFELL
SKAFTAFELL ○   ▲
                            This national-park headliner has trails aplenty, plus it's a stone's throw to Vatnajökull's icy treasures: glacier hikes, boat trips in ice-filled lagoons, snowmobiling and ice caves. (p34)
○ Kirkjubæjarklaustur

SKÓGAR

The area from Hella to Skógar is tops for horse riding, waterfalls and forays to Hekla or the famous Laugavegurinn trail, connecting Landmannalaugar and Þórsmörk. (p29)

Road Trips

1 The Golden Circle & the Southwest 2–3 Days
A stunning region of iconic wonders, including Iceland's historic parliament and the original geyser. (p21)

2 Southeast Iceland 3–4 Days
A captivatingly vast and surreal landscape dominated by mighty Vatnajökull ice cap. (p31)

3 East Iceland 2–3 Days
A quieter landscape of fishing villages, black-sand beaches, mountains and fjords. (p41)

4 North Iceland 4–5 Days
An epic ride northeast across geologically spectacular landscapes packed full of highlights. (p49)

5 West Iceland 1–2 Days
A compact tour through Saga country, from highland glaciers to ocean-fringed coastline near the capital. (p61)

Fjaðrárgljúfur (p32)

The Golden Circle & the Southwest

From black-sand Atlantic beaches, spouting geysers and glacier-fed waterfalls to brooding volcanoes and glittering ice caps, this remarkable region is waiting to awe you.

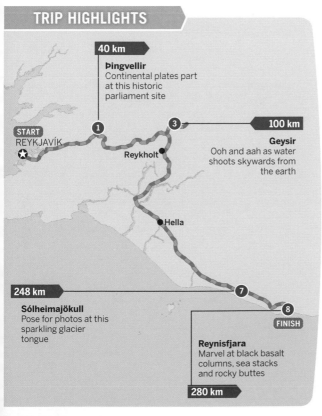

TRIP HIGHLIGHTS

40 km
Þingvellir
Continental plates part at this historic parliament site

START
REYKJAVÍK

Reykholt

100 km
Geysir
Ooh and aah as water shoots skywards from the earth

Hella

248 km
Sólheimajökull
Pose for photos at this sparkling glacier tongue

FINISH

Reynisfjara
Marvel at black basalt columns, sea stacks and rocky buttes

280 km

2–3 DAYS
280KM / 174 MILES

GREAT FOR...

BEST TIME TO GO
June to August is busy, but offers the best weather.

ESSENTIAL PHOTO
Black-sand beach at Reynisfjara with basalt-columned cliffs and puffins.

BEST FOR OUTDOORS
Hop between waterfalls cascading from volcanoes and ice caps along the Ring Road.

1

The Golden Circle & the Southwest

The southwest has many legendary natural wonders, and the further you go the better it gets. Faves such as Þingvellir, the former Icelandic parliament at the meeting of tectonic plates, are just beyond the capital. Churning seas lead to the Vestmannaeyjar archipelago. At the region's far reaches are the powerful Hekla and Eyjafjallajökull volcanoes, the adventure bases of Skógar and Vík, and the hidden valleys of Þórsmörk and Landmannalaugar.

TRIP HIGHLIGHT

❶ Þingvellir (p88)

Driving out of Reykjavík along the Ring Road through the capital's northern suburbs, mountains roll into view and the vistas expand. Turn east on Rte 36, passing through lush meadows marbled by clear streams to reach the dramatic rift valley of **Þingvellir National Park** (www.thingvellir. is; parking 300-500kr). One of the iconic stops on the Golden Circle route, Þingvellir is Iceland's most im-

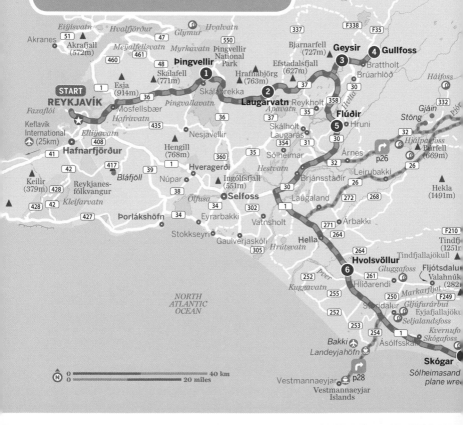

portant historical site and a place of vivid beauty. The Vikings established the world's first democratic parliament, the Alþingi (pronounced ál-thing-ee, also called Alþing), here in AD 930. The meetings were conducted outdoors and, as with many Saga sites, only the stone foundations of ancient encampments called *búðir* (literally 'booths') remain. The site has a superb natural setting, in an immense, fissured rift valley, caused by the meeting of the North American and Eurasian **tectonic plates**

(accessible via Rte 35 & Rte 361; parking 300kr), with rivers and waterfalls. Filling much of the rift plain south of the site, **Þingvallavatn** (accessible via Rte 361; parking 300kr) is Iceland's largest lake, at 84 sq km – the daring can dive into these glacial waters (in a dry suit).

From the Þingvellir Visitor Centre (p89) on Rte 36, at the top of **Almannagjá rift**, follow the path from the outlook down to the **Lögberg** (Law Rock; where the Alþingi convened annually) and the only standing structures in the great rift: a summerhouse and small **church** (☏482 2660; parking 300kr; ☺9am-5pm Jun-Aug) dating from 1859. You can also approach the waterfall **Öxarárfoss** from a parking area on Rte 36, and hike down into the rift valley from there. Or park on the eastern edge of the site (Rte 361).

The Drive » This 32km drive begins by tracing the edge of the foothills along Þingvallavatn lake. You'll start

on Rte 36, but turn east on Rte 365 to cut south of the dramatic mountains and emerge at Laugarvatn, both a lake and a village of the same name.

- - - - - - - - - - - - - - - - -

❷ Laugarvatn (p89)

Laugarvatn (Hot Springs Lake) is fed not only by streams running from the misty fells behind it, but by the hot spring Vígðalaug, famous since medieval times. A village, also called Laugarvatn, sits on the lake's western shore in the lap of the foothills. It is one of the better places to take a break on the Golden Circle. Unwind at **Fontana** (☏486 1400; www.fontana. is; Hverabraut 1; adult/child 3800/2000kr; ☺10am-11pm early Jun-late Aug, 11am-10pm late Aug-early Jun), a swanky lakeside soaking spot boasting three mod wading pools and a cedar-lined steam room that's fed by a naturally occurring vent below. The cafe has lake views. Or, if you're on a budget, hop into the municipal

> ## ✓ TOP TIP: BOOK AHEAD FOR LODGING
>
> It is absolutely essential to book well ahead for the summer season and on holidays, especially the further south you are going. There is simply not enough accommodation for the number of visitors, and hotels and guesthouses can be booked solid. It is not necessary to reserve ahead for campgrounds, but you will need your own equipment and sleeping bag.

LENGGIRL/SHUTTERSTOCK ©

geothermal pool (📞480 3041; Hverabraut 2; adult/child 1000/550kr; ⏰10am-9pm Mon-Fri, to 6pm Sat & Sun Jun–mid-Aug, shorter hours mid-Aug–May) next door.

The restaurant **Lindin** (📞486 1262; www.laugarvatn. is; Lindarbraut 2; mains 2200-5600kr; ⏰noon-10pm May-Sep, shorter hours Oct-Apr; 🅿🛜) is one of the best in the region and has both a casual bistro and a fine-dining lake-view wing in a sweet little silver house. Afterwards get a home-made ice cream while looking through viewing windows into the dairy barn at the farm of **Efstidalur II** (📞486 1186; www.efstidalur.is; Efstidalur 2; ice cream per scoop 500kr, mains 2250-5800kr; ⏰ice cream bar 10am-10pm, restaurant 11.30am-10pm; 🅿🛜), 12km northeast of town.

The Drive ≫ Leave Laugarvatn to the north along scenic Rte 37, which will wind you away from the lakeside foothills into increasingly open agricultural plains and then join up with Rte 35 to Geysir. As you approach Geysir (29km in total), you'll see first a geothermal outlet venting steam and then the ochre-seared Haukadalur geothermal area around the geyser.

TRIP HIGHLIGHT

❸ Geysir (p89)

One of Iceland's most famous tourist attractions, **Geysir** (Biskupstungna-braut; gay-zeer, literally 'gusher') is the original hot-water spout after which all other geysers

are named. The Great Geysir has been active for perhaps 800 years, and once gushed water up to 80m into the air. The geyser goes through periods of lessened activity, which seems to have been the case since 1916. Earthquakes can stimulate activity, but eruptions are rare. Luckily for visitors, the very reliable geyser **Strokkur** (Biskupstungnabraut) sits alongside. You rarely have to wait more than five to 10 minutes for the hot spring to shoot an impressive 15m to 30m plume before vanishing down its enormous hole.

The undulating, hissing geothermal area containing Geysir and Strokkur was free to enter at the time of writing, though there was discussion of instituting a fee. The large **Geysir Center** (📞519 6020; www.geysir center.com; ⏰9am-10pm Jun-Aug, to 6pm Sep-May; 🛜🍴) across the street from the geysers has cafes and restaurants, plus a shopping complex.

The Drive ≫ As you drive this short hop of only 10km along Rte 35 northeast to Gullfoss, stop and look back at the geothermal geyser area for a chance at great photos. Then follow the road as it dips alongside the vast, almost hidden, canyon of the Hvítá river north to the falls.

❹ Gullfoss (p91)

Iceland's most famous waterfall, **Gullfoss** (Golden Falls; www.gullfoss.is; Rte 35/ Kjalvegur) is a spectacular double cascade dropping a dramatic 32m back into the Hvítá river. As it descends, it kicks up brilliant walls of spray before thundering down a rocky ravine. On sunny days the mist creates shimmering rainbows, while in winter the falls glitter with ice. Although it's a popular sight, the remote location still makes you feel the ineffable forces of nature that have worked

Gullfoss

this landscape for millennia. Above the falls there's a small tourist information centre, shop and cafe.

If you'd like to approach the falls on horseback, book with **Geysir Hestar** (☎847 1046; www.geysirhestar.com; Kjóastaðir 2; ☺1/2/3hr rides 10,000/15,000/18,000kr), which offers horse riding for all skill levels and has one route along the river canyon to the falls. There are opportunities for rafting downriver from the falls with **Arctic Rafting** (☎562 7000; www.arcticraft ing.com; Drumboddsstaðir;

rafting/rafting & horse riding/ rafting & ATV tours per person from 19,000/30,000/34,000kr; ☺mid-May–mid-Sep) or with **Iceland Riverjet** (☎562 7000; www.icelandriverjet. com; Drumboddsstaðir; speed boat/Golden Circle & speed boat per person 14,900/20,000kr; ☺mid-Apr–Sep) in Reykholt.

The Drive >> The easiest route to Flúðir (35km) is to retrace your drive along Rte 35 to the junction with Rte 37, then turn south on Rte 35 along the western bank of the Hvítá, crossing the river on Rte 359 and continuing into Flúðir. Find Gamla Laugin lagoon signposted on the northern bank of the river Litla-Laxá in Flúðir.

⑤ Flúðir (p91)

Little agrarian Flúðir is known throughout Iceland for its geothermal greenhouses that grow the majority of the country's mushrooms, and it's also a popular weekend getaway for Reykjavikers with private cottages. More recently it's a super stop for its beautifully refurbished hot springs, **Gamla Laugin** (Secret Lagoon; ☎555 3351; www. secretlagoon.is; Hvammsvegur; adult/child 2800kr/free; ☺10am-10pm May-Sep, noon-8pm Oct-Apr). Soak in this broad, calm geothermal pool, mist rising and ringed by natural rocks. The walking trail along the edge of this lovely hot spring passes the local river and a series of sizzling vents and geysers. Surrounding meadows fill with wildflowers in summer. Increasingly popular, the lagoon gets packed with tour-bus crowds in mid-afternoon, so come early or late in the day.

To sample some of the local produce, stop in at **Flúðasveppir**

Farmers Bistro (📞519 0808; www.farmersbistro. is; Garðastígur; mains from 1900kr; 🕐 noon-6pm Jun-Aug, to 4pm Sep-May) about 3km northwest of town, which specialises in mushrooms. It offers the best produce of the region: veggies, meat, strawberries, rhubarb pie and bread, plus it has picnic tables out front.

The Drive » This 66km drive takes you south on Rte 30 for 31km to rejoin the Ring Road

(Rte 1) where you then turn east to the small town of Hvolsvöllur. Driving south out of Flúðir, the terrain becomes dramatic, with interesting rock buttes rising from rolling green plains. Back on the Ring Road, you'll pass lush horse farms.

- - - - - - - - - - - - - - - - - - - -

❻ Hvolsvöllur (p91)

The farms around Hvolsvöllur were the setting for the bloody events of *Njál's Saga*, one of Iceland's favourites. Today the Saga sites exist mainly as place names

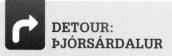

DETOUR: ÞJÓRSÁRDALUR

Start: ❺ **Flúðir**

The powerful Þjórsá is Iceland's longest river, a fast-flowing, churning mass of milky glacial water that courses 230km from Vatnajökull down to the Atlantic. Rte 32 follows the western side of the river and is easy to join at the junction with Rte 30, just south of Flúðir. As the road moves upstream into the highlands you'll traverse broad plains, split by the enormous river, that lead to volcanic fields and finally the foothills of the mountains beyond.

Continue 26km northeast to the short (1km) signposted track to delightful waterfall **Hjálparfoss**. The azure falls tumble in two chutes over twisted basalt columns and into a deep pool.

Next, make your way out to unique ruins at **Stöng**; a rough 5km dirt road branches off the other side of Rte 32 from Hjálparfoss. Buried by white volcanic ash in 1104 during one of Hekla's eruptions, the ancient farm at Stöng once belonged to Gaukur Trandilsson, a 10th-century Viking. Excavated in 1939 (Iceland's first proper archaeological dig), it's an important site, used to help date Viking houses elsewhere.

A path from Stöng takes you a couple of kilometres to the lush little valley of **Gjáin**, full of twisting lava, otherworldly caves and spectacular waterfalls. It was a filming location in *Game of Thrones*.

From Stöng you can also walk or take a 4WD 9km northeast along a track to Iceland's second-highest waterfall, **Háifoss**, which plunges 122m off the edge of a plateau into an undulating lava canyon.

Traverse the surreal black-stone river delta to Rte 26 to drive south and rejoin the Ring Road. Rte 26 passes alongside **Hekla**, one of Iceland's most ominous volcanoes, expected to erupt any day now.

TOURING THE HIGHLANDS

Landmannalaugar

Multicoloured mountains, soothing hot springs, rambling lava flows and clear blue lakes make Landmannalaugar one of Iceland's most unique destinations, and a must for explorers of the highlands. It's a favourite with Icelanders and visitors alike – as long as the weather cooperates. Part of the Fjallabak Nature Reserve, Landmannalaugar (600m above sea level) includes the largest geothermal field in Iceland outside the Grímsvötn caldera in Vatnajökull. Its multihued peaks are made of rhyolite – a mineral-filled lava that cooled unusually slowly, causing amazing colours. The area is the official starting point for the famous multiday Laugavegurinn hike to Þórsmörk, and there's excellent day hiking as well.

Þórsmörk

The hidden valley of Þórsmörk (*thors*-mork, literally 'Thor's Forest') sits at the confluence of several larger river-carved valleys. The protected area is a verdant realm of flower-filled lees that looks onto curling gorges, icy rivers and three looming glaciers (Tindfjallajökull, Eyjafjallajökull and Mýrdalsjökull). The glaciers protect this quiet spot from some of the region's harsher weather; it is often warmer or drier in Þórsmörk than nearby.

Getting There & Away

Both Landmannalaugar and Þórsmörk may seem relatively close to the Ring Road (Rte 1) on a map, but they can be tricky to reach. For Þórsmörk, especially, you'll need to take a bus or go by high-clearance 4WD (super-Jeep tour) to ford the rivers on the way to the reserve (or you can hike in from Skógar via the jaw-droppingly stunning Fimmvörðuháls hike). As you get close to Þórsmörk, you must cross sections and tributaries of the fast flowing Krossá river. Regular 4WDs cannot make it. You'll see that they are parked where people have hitched rides with buses or super-Jeeps. The best bet is to ditch your rental car at the Ring Road (Rte 1) and catch either a **Reykjavík Excursions** (Kynnisferðir; Map p74; ☑580 5400; www. re.is; BSÍ Bus Terminal, Vatnsmýrarvegur 10; tours 8000-47,300kr), **Sterna** (Map p78; ☑551 1166; www.sternatravel.com; Harpa Concert Hall, Austurbakki 2; ⊙7am-midnight Jun-Aug, 8am-10pm Sep-May) or **Trex** (☑587 6000; www.trex.is) bus, or book a tour with excellent local operators such as **Southcoast Adventure** (☑867 3535; www.southadventure.is; Hamragarðar Campground, Rte 249; 3/5hr tours from 22,900/32,900kr, price based on 2 people) or **Midgard Adventure** (☑578 3370; www.midgardadventure.is; Dufþaksbraut 14; tours 14,000-34,000kr).

---

or peaceful grassed-over ruins. The medieval turf-roofed farm at **Keldur** (☑530 2200; www.thjodmin jasafn.is; Rangárvallavegur/ Rte 264; admission 1200kr; ⊙10am-6pm mid-Jun–mid-Aug) is a historic settlement that once belonged to Ingjaldur Höskulds-son, a character in *Njál's*

Saga. About 5km west of Hvolsvöllur, unsurfaced Rte 264 winds about 8km north along the Rangárvellir valley to the pastoral site.

In Hvolsvöllur, the **LAVA – Iceland Volcano & Earthquake Centre** (☑415 5200; www.lavacentre. is; Austurvegur 14; adult/

child 2400kr/free, cinema only 1200kr/free, exhibition & cinema 3200kr; ⊙exhibition 9am-7pm, lava house to 9pm) has a full-blown multi-media experience immersing you in Iceland's volcanic and seismic life. To get out into this amazing terrain, hook up with Midgard Adventure, one of South Iceland's best bespoke adventure operators.

The Drive » After Hvolsvöllur, loop east for 49km on the Ring Road to Skógar. The drive brings you through broad plains carved by rivers and along the base of hulking Eyjafjallajökull, made famous by its ashy 2010 explosion. Views are magnificent on clear days, reaching to the ice caps of Eyjafjallajökull and Tindfjallajökull inland and the Vestmannaeyjar Islands offshore. Stop 22km along the way at thundering waterfall, Seljalandsfoss, which you can walk behind.

DETOUR: VESTMANNAEYJAR ISLANDS

Start: ⑥ Hvolsvöllur

East of Hvolsvöllur, Rte 254 shoots 12km south of the Ring Road to **Landeyjahöfn** where the **ferry** (☏481 2800; www.eimskip.is; Skildingav; per adult/child/bicycle/car 1380/760/690/2220kr) leaves for the 30-minute trip to the Vestmannaeyjar islands. Jagged and black, the Vestmannaeyjar (sometimes called the Westman Islands) form 15 eye-catching silhouettes off the southern shore. The islands were formed by submarine volcanoes around 11,000 years ago, except for Surtsey, the archipelago's newest addition, which rose from the waves in 1963.

Heimaey is the only inhabited Vestmannaeyjar island. It's famous for the 1973 eruption that almost smothered the town. The sheltered harbour lies between dramatic *klettur* (escarpments) and two ominous volcanoes – blood-red **Eldfell** and conical **Helgafell**. Heimaey is also known for its puffins (around 10 million birds come here to breed); make time to walk, cycle or drive around the island to see them, or take a boat tour with **Ribsafari** (☏661 1810; www.ribsafari.is; Básaskersbryggja 8, Harbour; 1hr tour adult/child 11,900/6500kr, 2hr 17,950/9500kr; ☉mid-Apr–Oct) or **Viking Tours** (☏488 4884; www.vikingtours.is; Strandvegur 65; adult/child boat trips from 7400/6400kr, bus trips from 6400/5400kr; ☉10am-6pm May–mid-Sep).

The state-of-the-art volcano museum **Eldheimar** (Pompeii of the North; ☏488 2700; www.eldheimar.is; Gerðisbraut 10; adult/child 2300/1200kr; ☉11am-6pm) is a must-visit. More than 400 buildings lie buried under lava from the 1973 eruption, and on the edge of the flow this museum revolves around one house excavated from 50m of pumice. The museum allows a glimpse into the home, with its crumbling walls and intact but toppled knick-knacks, and is filled with multimedia exhibits on the eruption and its aftermath.

Lovely seaside 15th-century fort **Skansinn** was built to defend the harbour (not too successfully, though – when Algerian pirates arrived in 1627, they simply landed on the other side of the island).

Kids might enjoy **Sæheimar** (☏481 1997; www.saeheimar.is; Heiðarvegur 12; adult/10-17yr/up to 9yr 1200/500kr/free; ☉10am-5pm May-Sep, 1-4pm Sat Oct-Apr; ♿), an aquarium and natural history museum where there's often a real-life puffin wobbling about – the museum is an informal bird hospital.

If time permits, eat at **Slippurinn** (☏481 1515; www.slippurinn.com; Strandvegur 76; lunch 2400-7200kr, dinner mains 3700-4900kr, set menu 6400-9900kr; ☉noon-2.30pm & 5-10pm early May–mid-Sep; 🛜), one of the best restaurants in Iceland for high-concept Icelandic fare, or grab a bite before your ferry at harbourside **Tanginn** (☏414 4420; www.facebook.com/tanginn.is; Básaskersbryggja 8; mains 2200-3000kr; ☉11.30am-9.30pm Sun-Wed, to 1pm Thu, to 2pm Fri & Sat; 🛜♿).

❼ Skógar (p92)

Skógar nestles under the **Eyjafjallajökull** ice cap just north of the Ring Road. This little tourist settlement is the start (or occasionally end) of the hike over the Fimmvörðuháls pass to Þórsmörk, and is one of the activities centres of the Southwest. At its western edge, you'll see the dizzying 62m waterfall **Skógafoss**. Climb the steep staircase alongside for giddy views, or walk to the foot of the falls, shrouded in sheets of mist and rainbows. Legend has it that a settler named Þrasi hid a chest of gold behind Skógafoss...

On the eastern side of town, the fantastic **Skógar Folk Museum** (Skógasafn; ☎487 8845; www.skogasafn.is; Skógavegur, near Rte 1; adult/child 2000kr/ free; ☉9am-6pm Jun-Aug, 10am-5pm Sep-May) covers all aspects of Icelandic life, with extensive exhibits, restored buildings (a church, a turf-roofed farmhouse, cowsheds), and a huge, modern building containing a transport and communication museum.

From Skógar, it's also easy to join a guided walk on one of the easiest glacial tongues to reach: **Sólheimajökull**. This icy outlet glacier unfurls from the main **Mýrdalsjökull** ice cap and is a favourite spot for glacial walks and ice climbing. Rte 221 leads 4.2km off the Ring Road to a small car park from where you can walk the 800m to the ice along a wide track edging the glacial lagoon. Don't attempt to climb onto the glacier unguided – contact **Arcanum** (☎487 1500; www.arcanum.is; glacier walks from 9500kr, ATV tours from 19,000kr, snowmobile rides per 2 people from 27,000kr; ☉9.30am-5pm), **Icelandic Mountain Guides** (☎587 9999, Skógar desk 894 2956; www.mountainguides.is; glacier kayaking from 12,900kr, guided Fimmvörðuháls hikes from 89,900kr; ☉9.30am-5pm) or **Mountain Excursion** (☎897 7737; www.mountainexcursion.is; glacier hikes from 10,500kr, super-Jeep tours from 21,500kr; ☉9am-5pm).

The Drive ❯❯ As the Ring Road arcs 33km east from Skógar to Vík, the haunches of the foothills rise to glaciers, mountaintops and volcanoes inland, while rivers descend from mysterious gorges and course across the broad sweep of pastures to black-sand beaches and the crashing ocean.

❽ Vík (p92)

The welcoming little community of Vík (aka Vík í Mýrdal) has become a booming hub for a beautiful portion of the South Coast. Iceland's southernmost town, it's also the rainiest, but that doesn't stop the madhouse atmosphere in summer, when every room within 100km is booked solid. On the western side of **Reynisfjall** (340m), the high ridge above Vík, Rte 215 leads 5km down to black-sand beach **Reynisfjara**. It's backed by an incredible stack of basalt columns that look like a magical church organ, and there are outstanding views west to Dyrhólaey. Surrounding cliffs are pocked with caves formed from twisted basalt, and puffins belly flop into the crashing sea during summer. Immediately offshore are the towering **Reynisdrangur** sea stacks. Tradition says they're masts of a ship that trolls were stealing when they got caught in the sun. At all times watch for rogue waves: people are regularly swept away.

One of the South Coast's most recognisable natural formations is the rocky plateau and huge stone sea arch at **Dyrhólaey** (deer-lay), which rises dramatically from the surrounding plain 10km west of Vík, at the end of Rte 218. Visit its crashing black beaches and get awesome views from atop the promontory. The islet is a nature reserve rich in bird life, including puffins. Be aware that some or all of it can be closed during nesting season. (15 May to 25 June) to protect the offspring.

Southeast Iceland

2

The mighty Vatnajökull ice cap dominates the Southeast, its huge rivers of frozen ice pouring down steep-sided valleys toward the sea, like icing on a cake. Vistas are vast and otherworldly.

TRIP HIGHLIGHTS

227 km

Route F985
Take a hair-raising snowmobile ride, 840m above sea level

140 km

Skaftafell
The jewel in the crown of Vatnajökull National Park

10 Höfn **FINISH**

8

5

6

192 km

Jökulsárlón
Boat around the ice sculptures of a captivating lagoon

START Vík

165 km

Ingólfshöfði
Tour an offshore promontory rich in panoramas and birdlife

3–4 DAYS
272KM / 169 MILES

GREAT FOR...

BEST TIME TO GO
Hiking from June to September; ice caves from mid-November to March.

ESSENTIAL PHOTO
The luminous blue icebergs of Jökulsárlón ice lagoon.

BEST FOR FOODIES
Tuck into locally caught langoustine in Höfn.

Jökulsárlón Icebergs drifting to sea (p37)

2 Southeast Iceland

The 200km stretch of Ring Road from Kirkjubæjarklaustur to Höfn is mind-blowing, transporting you across stark deltas of grey glacial sand, past lost-looking farms, around the toes of craggy mountains and alongside glacier tongues and ice-filled lagoons. The only thing you won't pass is a town – but there are properties offering brilliant activities, accommodation and meals (book well ahead, as beds here are in hot demand).

❶ Fjaðrárgljúfur

The route east from Vík is a scenic delight, with the Reynisdrangur sea stacks receding in the rear-view mirror while you traverse **Mýrdalssandur** outwash plain, formed from eruptions of the Katla volcano, and then **Eldhraun**, remarkable moss-covered lava fields created by the epic Laki eruptions of 1783.

After about 65km, take the turn north on Rte 206 and follow the road for 3km to reach Fjaðrárgljúfur, a darkly

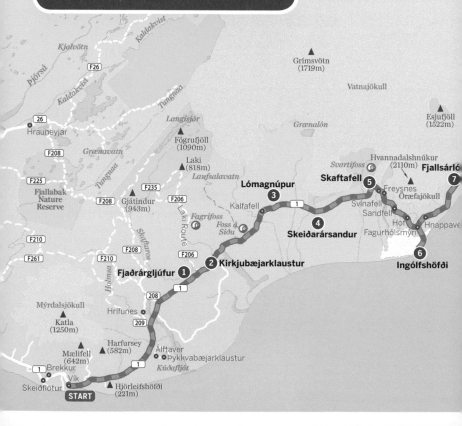

picturesque canyon carved out by the river Fjaðrá. A walking track follows its southern edge for a couple of kilometres, with plenty of places to gaze down into its rocky depths.

The Drive 》 Return to the Ring Road and continue east – it's 6km until you reach the junction with Kirkjubæjarklaustur. En route, note the vast, dimpled, vivid-green pseudocrater field (known as Landbrotshólar) south of the Ring Road. Pseudocraters formed when hot lava poured over wetlands; the subsurface water boiled and steam exploded through to make these barrowlike mounds.

----

❷ Kirkjubæjar-klaustur (p93)

Many a foreign tongue has been tied in knots trying to say Kirkjubæjarklaustur. The name translates as 'church-farm-cloister', and the locals simply call it 'Klaustur' (pronounced like 'cloister'). The town is tiny, even by Icelandic standards – a few houses and farms scattered across a brilliant green backdrop. Still, it's the only real service town between Vík and Höfn, so stop for petrol and groceries, and to explore some cool anomalies and top-notch walks. The basalt columns of **Kirkjugólf**, smoothed down and cemented with moss, were once mistaken for an old church floor rather than a work of nature, and it's easy to see why. The honeycombed slab lies in a field about 400m northwest of the N1 petrol station (drive down Rte 203 for access). At the western end of the village, **Systrafoss** (Sisters' Falls) is a lovely double waterfall. The lake **Systravatn**, a short saunter up the cliffs beside the waterfall, was once a bathing place for nuns.

The Drive 》 About 11km from Klaustur you'll pass waterfall Foss á Síðu tumbling down from the cliffs. Just east of the waterfall is the outcrop Dverghamrar (Dwarf Rocks) – two rock formations that feature classic basalt columns and are thought to be the dwelling place of some of Iceland's 'hidden people'. From here the road marches on, past emerald green landscapes interspersed with gravelly riverbeds.

----

❸ Lómagnúpur (p93)

Adding eye candy to an impressive road trip, a precipitous 767m-tall palisade of cliffs known as Lómagnúpur towers distinctively over the

Hoffellsjökull 13

Ketillaugarfjall (670m)

Lonsvik

Fláajökull

Heinabergslón Hólmur

Bjarnanes

Brunnhorn (575m)

11 Höfn 14

Vestrahorn (575m)

inabergsjökull

F985 10

Hornafjörður FINISH Stokksnes

Route F985

Hali

Kalfatellsstadhur

Jökulsárlón

NORTH ATLANTIC OCEAN

0 —————————— 40 km
0 —————————— 20 miles

landscape. It's full of legends and looks particularly good as a backdrop to the old turf-roofed farm at **Núpsstaður** just to its west. The farm buildings date from the early 19th century, and the idyllic chapel is one of Iceland's last turf churches. Note that you can't drive onto the property, but you can park by the road and walk up to the buildings to take photos.

The Drive >> As you continue east, you'll encounter Skeiðarársandur, a barren outwash plain stretching some 50km. It's a flat expanse of barren grey-black sands, fierce scouring winds and fast-flowing glacial rivers.

----

4 Skeiðarársandur

The sandar are eerily flat and empty regions sprawling along Iceland's southern coast. High in the mountains, glaciers scrape up silt, sand and gravel, which is then carried by glacial rivers or (more dramatically) by glacial bursts down to the coast and dumped in huge, desertlike plains. The sandar here are so impressively huge

that the Icelandic word (singular: sandur) is used internationally to describe the topographic phenomenon of a glacial outwash plain.

Skeiðarársandur, the largest sandur in the world, covers a 1300-sq-km area and was formed by the Skeiðarárjökull glacier. Since the Settlement Era, Skeiðarársandur has swallowed a considerable amount of farmland and it continues to grow.

The section of Ring Road that crosses Skeiðarársandur was the last bit of the national highway to be constructed, in 1974 (until then, residents of Höfn had to drive to Reykjavík via Akureyri in the north).

The Drive >> As you traverse the sandur, note the long gravel dykes that have been strategically positioned to channel floodwaters. They did little good, however, when in late 1996 three bridges were washed away like matchsticks by a massive jökulhlaup (glacial flood). There's a memorial of twisted bridge girders and an information board just west of Skaftafell.

CANADASTOCK/SHUTTERSTOCK ©

TRIP HIGHLIGHT

5 Skaftafell (p95)

Skaftafell, the jewel in the crown of Vatnajökull National Park (p36), encompasses a breathtaking collection of peaks and glaciers. It's the country's favourite wilderness: annually, more than half a million visitors come to marvel at thundering waterfalls, twisted birch woods, the tangled web of rivers threading across the sandar, and the crevasse-pleated outlet glaciers flowing down from the

----

ICY ACTIVITIES

Activities that explore the icy vastness of Vatnajökull (p36) – glacier walks, super-Jeep tours, lagoon boat tours and snowmobile safaris – are accessed along the Ring Road between Skaftafell and Höfn.

Turf-roofed farmhouse near Skaftafell

immense Vatnajökull ice cap.

The Skaftafellsstofa Visitor Centre (p96) has exhibitions and a cafe, and oversees a large campground. Helpful rangers provide maps and information on park attractions and glorious trails; nearby activity companies offer glacier walks and more.

Star of a hundred postcards, **Svartifoss** (Black Falls) is a stunning, moody-looking waterfall flanked by geometric black basalt columns. It's reached by a relatively easy 1.8km trail lead-

ing up from the visitor centre. Another popular option is the easy one-hour return walk (3.7km) to **Skaftafellsjökull**. The marked trail begins at the visitor centre and leads to the glacier face.

The Drive » The unfolding landscape of glittering glaciers and brooding mountains makes it difficult to keep your eyes on the road. On clear days, look for the peak of Iceland's highest mountain, Hvannadalshnúkur (2110m). The signposted departure point for Ingólfshöfði tours is about 25km east of Skaftafell at Fagurhólsmýri (drive south to the tour departure hut, 2km off the Ring Road).

- - - - - - - - - - - - - - - -

TRIP HIGHLIGHT

⑥ Ingólfshöfði (p96)

While everyone's gaze naturally turns inland in this spectacular part of Iceland, there are reasons to look offshore, too – in particular to the 76m-high Ingólfshöfði promontory, rising from the flatlands like a strange dream.

In spring and summer, this beautiful, isolated nature reserve is overrun with nesting puffins, skuas and other seabirds. It's also of great historical importance – it was here that Ingólfur Arnarson, Iceland's first settler, stayed the winter on his original foray to the country in AD 874.

Tours (☏894 0894; www.puffintour.is; adult/child 7500/2500kr; ☉10.15am & 1.30pm Mon-Sat mid-May–mid-Aug) of Ingólfshöfði begin with a fun ride across 6km of shallow tidal lagoon (in a tractor-drawn wagon), then a short but steep sandy climb, followed by a 1½-hour guided walk round the flat headland. The emphasis is on birdwatching, with stunning mountain backdrops to marvel over. Note that puffins usually

leave around mid-August. Confirm times via the website, where you can also book tickets.

The Drive » More ice-tinted landscapes await, to fill your 20-minute drive to the next stop.

----

❼ Fjallsárlón

A sign off the Ring Road indicates Fjallsárlón – this is an easily accessible glacier lagoon, considerably less famous than busy Jökulsárlón, 10km further east.

If you have the time, stop at both lagoons to admire their different features: Jökulsárlón is much larger and more dramatic, while from

Fjallsárlón's shores you can see the glacier snout (icebergs calve from Fjallsjökull outlet glacier). There are lovely walks at each site, and both lagoons offer boat rides. Fjallsárlón wins brownie points for building a handsome visitor centre, with cafe. Check out **Fjallsárlón Glacial Lagoon Boat Tours** (☏666 8006; www.fjallsarlon. is; adult/child 6900/3500kr; ☉May-Oct) for information.

The Drive » It's only 10km from Fjallsárlón to Jökulsárlón, which sits right beside the Ring Road; even when you're driving along, expecting this surreal scene, it's still a gorgeous visual

VATNAJÖKULL NATIONAL PARK

Vast, varied and spectacular, Vatnajökull National Park was founded in 2008, when authorities created a giant megapark by joining the Vatnajökull ice cap with two previously established national parks: Skaftafell in Southeast Iceland and Jökulsárgljúfur in the northeast. The park now measures over 14,100 sq km – approximately 14% of the entire country (it's one of the largest national parks in Europe). It has been nominated for inclusion on the Unesco World Heritage list.

The park boundaries encircle a staggering richness of landscapes and some of Iceland's greatest natural treasures, created by the combined forces of rivers, glacial ice, and volcanic and geothermal activity (yes, fire-and-ice cliché alert!). The entirety of the Vatnajökull ice cap is protected, including countless glistening outlet glaciers and glacial rivers. There are incredible waterfalls such as Dettifoss and Svartifoss, the storied Lakagígar crater row, Askja and other volcanoes of the highlands, and an unending variety of areas where geology, ecology and history lessons spring to life.

The park's website (www.vjp.is) is filled with important information – details on trails, campsites, access roads etc, plus it has downloadable maps and brochures. There are useful visitor centres in the Southeast in the towns of Kirkjubæjarklaustur (p93) and Höfn (p97), and at Skaftafell (p96).

Hiking trails and 4WD routes can get you to remote gems, but you don't have to get off the beaten track to sample some of the park's highlights – in fact, quite a few worthy diversions (and awesome vistas) can be accessed from a standard Ring Road journey of the country, and there's a smorgasbord of tour offerings.

Boat tour on Fjallsárlón glacier lagoon

surprise. Be careful – there's a single-lane bridge here, and lots of distracted drivers!

- - - - - - - - - - - - - - - - - -

TRIP HIGHLIGHT

⑧ Jökulsárlón

One of Iceland's most magical sights, Jökulsárlón glacier lagoon is filled with spectacular, luminous blue icebergs drifting out to sea. You'll be wowed by the wondrous ice sculptures as they spin in the changing light; you can also scout for seals in the lagoon, and take a boat trip.

The icebergs calve from Breiðamerkurjökull glacier, an offshoot of Vatnajökull. They can spend up to five years floating in the 25-sq-km-plus, 250m-deep lagoon, melting, refreezing and occasionally toppling over with a mighty splash, startling the birds. They then move on via **Jökulsá**, Iceland's shortest river, out to sea.

Take a memorable 40-minute trip with **Glacier Lagoon Amphibious Boat Tours** (☑478 2222; www.icelagoon.is; adult/child 5700/2000kr; ⊙9am-7pm Jun-Sep, 10am-5pm May & Oct), the vehicles of which trundle along the shore like buses before driving into the water. It also offers Zodiac tours, as does **Ice Lagoon Zodiac Boat Tours** (☑860 9996; www.icelagoon.com; adult/child 9700/6200kr; ⊙9am-5.30pm May-Sep), which speed up to the glacier edge (not done by the amphibious boats) before cruising back slowly. Check online for details and to book ahead.

The Drive » Before leaving Jökulsárlón, visit the river mouth (there are car parks on the ocean side of the Ring Road), where you'll see ice boulders resting photogenically on the black-sand 'Diamond Beach' as

TOP TIP: LOCAL BEER

We're suckers for a good sales pitch, and Vatnajökull Beer has it in spades: 'frozen in time' beer brewed from 1000-year-old water (ie Jökulsárlón icebergs), flavoured with locally grown Arctic thyme. It's sold in restaurants around the Southeast. Give it a try for its fruity, malty flavour.

part of their final journey out to sea. It's only a short hop (14km) from Jökulsárlón to the tiny settlement of Hali.

➒ Hali (p96)

There's a small cluster of in-demand accommodation at Hali, the closest settlement to Jökulsárlón. Here you'll also find **Þórbergssetur** (📞478 1078; www.thorbergur. is; adult/child 1000kr/free; ☉9am-8pm), a cleverly crafted museum (its inspired exterior looks like a shelf of books) that pays tribute to the most famous son of this sparsely populated region – writer Þórbergur Þórðarson (1888–1974). Þórbergssetur also functions as a kind of cultural centre, with changing art exhibitions and a quality **cafe-restaurant** (📞478 1078; www.hali.is/ restaurant; mains lunch 1550-3100kr, dinner 3200-5500kr; ☉11am-9pm) specialising in locally caught Arctic char.

The Drive » The super-scenic stretch of Ring Road between Hali and Höfn is 66km in length,

and home to around 20 rural properties (many with glaciers in their backyards) offering accommodation, activities and occasionally food. About 21km east of Hali, the F985 track branches north to the broad glacial spur Skálafellsjökull.

TRIP HIGHLIGHT

➓ Route F985

This dramatic 16km-long road is practically vertical in places, and is for large 4WDs and confident drivers only. Don't even think of attempting to drive Rte F985 in a 2WD car – you'll end up with a huge rescue bill. Instead, take a ride with one of the companies that drive tourists up the road and then guide them on icy endeavours.

At the end of Rte F985, 840m above sea level and with spectacular 360-degree views, most travellers choose to do an awesome **snowmobile ride**. You're kitted out with overalls, helmets, boots and gloves, and play follow-the-leader along a fixed trail. It's great fun, but if the skidoo isn't your thing you

can also take a super-Jeep ride onto the ice.

Contact **Glacier Jeeps** (📞894 3133, 478 1000; www. glacierjeeps.is; ☉Mar–mid-Oct), which does summer pick-up from the small car park at the corner of the Ring Road and Rte F985, or **Glacier Journey** (📞478 1517; www.glacierjour ney.is), which operates from Flatey á Mýrum in summer; in winter, Glacier Journey's base is at Jökulsárlón.

The Drive » Once back on the Ring Road, you'll pass a turn-off to a cluster of guesthouses, and then a sign indicating Heinabergsjökull, a glacier tongue reached after 8km on gravel. It pays to ask locally about the condition of the road before setting off in a 2WD.

⓫ Heinabergsjökull

Vatnajökull National Park authorities are working with a handful of landowners between Jökulsárlón and Höfn to open up public access to areas of raw natural beauty. These areas are signed off the Ring Road – for now, they are not especially well known, so you stand a good chance of finding yourself a tranquil pocket of glaciated wonder.

Heinabergsjökull has lovely walks, and you can go on brilliant summertime kayaking trips on the icy lagoon (called Heinabergslón) at its snout. The trips are operated by **IceGuide** (📞661 0900; www.iceguide.is).

The Drive » Rejoin the Ring Road and continue 11km east (past a lookout point) to reach Hólmur.

The Drive » About 15km east of Hólmur farm is a sign pointing the way north to Hoffell guesthouse.

⑫ Hólmur

A perfect pit stop for families, **Hólmur** (📞478 2063; www.holmurinn. is; s/d without bathroom from 10,800/14,000kr; 🛜) farm offers well-priced farmhouse accommodation and a sweet **farm zoo** (adult/child 900/700kr; 🕐Jun-Sep) with an abundance of feathered and furry friends. Also here is a stand-out restaurant, Jón Ríki (p96).

The glacier tongue **Fláajökull** is 8km off the Ring Road on a gravel road, signposted just east of Hólmur. A suspension bridge here (which gave front-row views of the glacier to walkers) was washed away in 2017 floods but there are plans to rebuild. Glacier walks are operated on Fláajökull, led by **Glacier Trips** (📞779 2919; www.glaciertrips. is; glacier walk 19,900kr) – this is a great alternative to Skaftafell-area glacier walks, as Fláajökull sees few tourists.

⑬ Hoffellsjökull

En route to the **Hoffell** (Glacier World; 📞478 1514; www.glacierworld.is; d with/ without bathroom incl breakfast 31,100/21,000kr; 🛜) guesthouse, a signed, 4km gravel road leads to Hoffellsjökull glacier tongue, calving into a small lake. There are some good short walks in the area, plus longer hikes.

The most popular reason to stop by the Hoffell guesthouse is the chance to soak in a collection of geothermally heated outdoor **hot-pots** (per person 1000kr; 🕐10am-8pm).

The Drive » Head back to the Ring Road to drive the final 17km to Höfn. You'll need to take the turn-off south of the Ring Road, travelling on Rte 99 for the final 6km.

⑭ Höfn (p96)

Although it's no bigger than many European villages, the Southeast's main town feels like a sprawling metropolis

after driving through the emptiness on either side. Its setting is stunning; on a clear day, wander along to the waterside, find a quiet bench and just gaze at Vatnajökull and its brotherhood of glaciers.

There are good areas for panorama-filled walks, including around the marshes and lagoons at the end of the promontory **Ósland** (about 1km beyond the harbour – head for the seamen's monument on the rise). The area is great for watching seabirds, though watch out for dive-bombing Arctic terns.

'Höfn' simply means 'harbour', and is pronounced like an unexpected hiccup (just say 'hup' while inhaling). The town relies heavily on fishing and fish processing, and is famous for its *humar* (langoustine). Come mealtime, the hottest tables are at innovative harbourside **Pakkhús** (📞478 2280; www.pakkhus.is; Krosseyjarvegur 3; mains 3100-6790kr; 🕐noon-10pm).

East Iceland

As far as you can get from Reykjavík, Iceland's sparsely populated east doesn't announce itself as loudly as other parts of the country, preferring subtle charms over big-ticket attractions.

TRIP HIGHLIGHTS

256 km

Egilsstaðir
Easy escapes to lakeshore diversions or arty fjord towns

8 FINISH

183 km

Stöðvarfjörður
Sparking stones and minerals, handicrafts and more creativity

5

104 km

Djúpivogur
Slow living, artistic flavour, and the chance to visit puffins

2

16 km

Stokksnes
Black-sand beaches, moody mountain backdrops and a Viking film set

START
Höfn **1**

2–3 DAYS
256KM / 159 MILES

GREAT FOR...

BEST TIME TO GO
June to August sees the region in full swing, with the best chance of good weather.

 ESSENTIAL PHOTO
The black-sand beach at Stokksnes, backed by Vestrahorn peak.

 BEST FOR WILDLIFE
Take a boat tour from Djúpivogur to Papey for seals and seabirds.

Djúpivogur Historic port town (p47)

3 East Iceland

Most travellers hit the accelerator and follow the over-eager Ring Road as it ploughs through the east, but they're missing some gems. This is a region that rewards slow travel: prepare yourself for superb vistas as the road skirts mountain peaks, steep-sided fjords, black-sand beaches and broad valleys. Stop to admire tiny fishing villages bathed in creativity and to investigate ancient geology.

❶ Stokksnes

From Höfn, rejoin the Ring Road (Rte 1) heading east, and after about 7km, just before the Ring Road enters a tunnel through the Almannaskarð pass, take the signposted road south to Stokksnes cape. After 4.5km, in a wild setting under moodily Gothic Vestrahorn mountain, you'll find a cool little outpost: the **Viking Cafe** (☎478 2577; www.vikingcafe.is; snacks & meals

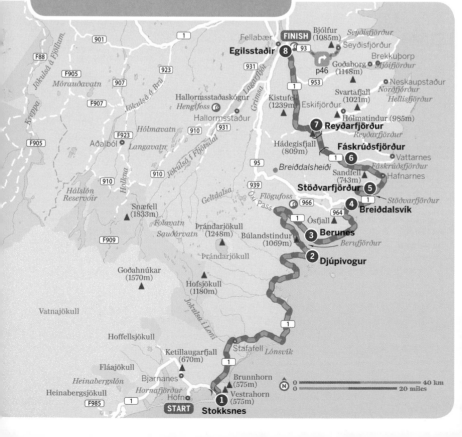

700-1500kr), where coffee, waffles and cake are served. Rooms are also offered.

The farm-owner runs the cafe, and he charges visitors a small fee (800kr) to explore his incredible property, including a photogenic Viking village film set (built by Icelandic movie director Baltasar Kormákur in 2009 but yet to be used for its intended purpose) and miles of black-sand beaches, where seals laze and the backdrop of Vestrahorn creates superb photos.

The Drive » Rejoin the Ring Road and head north. The 104km stretch around Iceland's southeast corner, between Höfn and Djúpivogur, is another impossibly scenic stretch, the road curving past only a handful of farms backed by precipitous peaks, plus black-sand beaches and a swan-filled lagoon at Hvalnes Nature Reserve, where you can stop and stretch your legs. Note: no fuel stops, very limited toilet facilities.

TRIP HIGHLIGHT

❷ Djúpivogur (p97)

Djúpivogur's historic buildings, artists' workshops and small harbour are worth a look, but the main reason to visit this friendly fishing village is to catch the boat to **Papey**, a small offshore island inhabited only by sunbathing seals and nesting seabirds, including a puffin posse. There are usually boat tours

to the island departing Djúpivogur harbour daily June to August.

Djúpivogur is actually one of the oldest ports in the country – it's been around since the 16th century, when German merchants brought goods to trade. These days the town has embraced the Cittaslow movement ('Slow Cities'), an offshoot of the Slow Food initiative, and there's a low-key, creative vibe and some alfresco art worth checking out, including **Eggin í Gleðivík**: 34 oversized eggs along the jetty, each one representing a local bird. A few quirky artisans work with local stones and driftwood to create jewellery or artful objects, such as **JFS Handcraft** (Hammersminni 10; ⊗10am-6pm).

The Drive » The Ring Road meanders around Berufjörður, a long, steep-sided fjord. The southwestern shore is dominated by the pyramid-shaped mountain Búlandstindur, rising 1069m above the water.

There's also a nature reserve, Teigarhorn, renowned for zeolite crystals and home to some short walks.

❸ Berunes

Looking to break your journey somewhere remote and scenic? **Berunes HI Hostel** (📞869 7227, 478 8988; www.berunes. is; dm/d without bathroom 6600/16,200kr, cottages from 22,620kr; ⊗Apr-Oct; @🛜) is on a century-old farm run by affable Ólafur and his family. There are rooms in a wonderfully creaky old farmhouse plus newer buildings, and also a campsite and cottages. There's a summer evening restaurant, too.

On the farm next to Berunes is **Havarí** (📞663 5520; www.havari. is; Karlsstaðir; meals 800-2000kr; ⊗8am-9pm May-Sep, shorter hours Oct-Apr; 🛜📞), a warm, creative place owned by a young family that includes acclaimed musician Prins Póló. A converted barn is now a

PAPEY

The name of offshore island Papey (Friars' Island) suggests it was once a hermitage for the Irish monks who may have briefly inhabited Iceland before fleeing upon the arrival of the Norse. This small (2 sq km) and tranquil island was once a farm, but it's now uninhabited. As well as the local wildlife (puffins can be easily spotted from mid-April to early/mid-August), other highlights include the rock Kastali (the Castle), home to the 'hidden people'; a lighthouse built in 1922; and Iceland's oldest and smallest wooden church (from 1807).

cafe and live-music venue – look out for events on Havarí's Facebook page, or stop by to try tasty farm-made *bulsur* (vegan sausages). You can also order great coffee, soup and waffles. Also here: a cosy hostel building. Winter hours for Havarí are less concrete – call, or check Facebook.

The Drive » Follow the road as it skirts around Ósfjall mountain and runs along the impressive black-sand beach of Meleyri. The view west of here takes in Breiðdalur ('Broad Valley'). Take a signed right turn to reach Breiðdalsvík.

---

4 Breiðdalsvík (p97)

The tiny fishing village of Breiðdalsvík is beautifully positioned at the end of Breiðdalur. It's a quiet place – more a base for walking in the nearby hills and fishing the rivers and lakes than an attraction in itself. Stop by **Kaupfjélagið** (☏475 6670; www.facebook.com/kaupfjelagid; Sólvellir 23; light meals 370-1650kr; ◷10am-7pm Mon-Thu, to 8pm Fri & Sat, to 5pm Sun), the general store, for coffee and a bite. Its best features are the fun displays of vintage general-store items that were discovered in the attic during recent renovations.

The town's newest addition is a fun microbrewery, and it's drawing curious travellers with its genial nature and quaffable brews. Opened in 2016, **Beljandi Brugghús** (☏860 9905; www.facebook.com/beljandibrugghus; Sólvellir 23; ◷11am-11.45pm Fri-Wed Jun-Aug, shorter hours rest of year) has free samples of its concoctions: the signature Beljandi is a pale ale. The bar area hosts occasional events (live music, big-screen sports) and the chance to imbibe more options. This is another place where opening hours can be erratic, so it pays to check (via Facebook or a phone call).

The Drive » From Breiðdalsvík you need to determine your preferred route to Egilsstaðir: west over a mountain road (Rte 95; 83km; often closed in winter), or east along the fjord-side route (92km). Since late 2017, the Ring Road has followed the scenic waterside path.

SIMONE GRAMEGNA/SHUTTERSTOCK ©

LOCAL EXPERIENCES

With its small population (around 11,000), distance from the capital, and with the Ring Road steaming quickly through it, East Iceland has struggled to get the traveller attention it deserves. **Tanni Travel** (☏476 1399; www.meetthelocals.is) aims to change that, and works with locals to create unique experiences. The agency is based in Eskifjörður but works all over the east, and offers summertime guided village walks, plus it can devise itineraries (themed from local food to 'nostalgic Christmas') and put you in touch with activity providers (which can be particularly useful in winter). Unique in Iceland, it also offers travellers the chance to spend an evening dining in the home of locals (per adult/child 15,300/7650kr).

Vestrahorn and the beach at Stokksnes (p42)

TRIP HIGHLIGHT

⑤ Stöðvarfjörður

If you think geology is boring, it's worth challenging that notion in this tiny village, which the Ring Road now cruises right through. It's a small place, but it has built a sizeable reputation for both its stone collection and its creativity. Look out for what may be the country's cutest **bird hide** at the head of the fjord, as you motor into town.

The wondrous assemblage at **Steinasafn Petru** (☎475 8834; www.steina petra.is; Fjarðarbraut 21; adult/child 1500kr/free; ⊙9am-6pm May–mid-Oct), or Petra's Mineral Collection, was a lifelong labour of love for Petra Sveinsdóttir (1922–2012). Inside her house, stones and minerals are piled from floor to ceiling – 70% of them are from the local area. They include beautiful cubes of jasper, polished agate, purple amethyst, glowing creamy 'ghost stone', glittering quartz crystals...it's like opening a treasure chest.

The Drive » The road skirts a mountainous arm of land as it reaches for the next fjord. Geologists may get a buzz from the lacolithic mountain Sandfell (743m), which was formed by molten rhyolite bursting through older lava layers. It's one of the world's finest examples of this sort of igneous mountain. Feeling energetic? It's a four-hour return hike to peak.

⑥ Fáskrúðsfjörður

The sleepy village of Fáskrúðsfjörður (sometimes known as Búðir) was originally settled by French seamen who came to fish the Icelandic coast between the late 19th century and 1914. In a gesture to local heritage, street signs are in both Icelandic and French.

45

DETOUR: SEYÐISFJÖRÐUR

Start: ⑧ **Egilsstaðir**

If you explore only one town in the Eastfjords, Seyðisfjörður should be it. Made up of multicoloured wooden houses and surrounded by snowcapped mountains and cascading waterfalls, obscenely picturesque Seyðisfjörður is the most historically and architecturally interesting town in East Iceland. It's also a friendly place with an international community of artists, musicians, craftspeople and students.

There are fun hiking trails and activity options, great places to stay and superb eating options – try the super-fresh sushi at **Norð Austur Sushi & Bar** (📞787 4000; www.nordaustur.is; 2nd fl, Norðurgata 2; small dishes 690-2190kr; maki rolls 2190-2690kr; ⊙5-10pm Sun-Thu, to 11pm Fri & Sat Jun-early Sep) or pizzas at **Skaftfell** (📞472 1633; http:// skaftfell.is/en/bistro; Austurvegur 42; pizzas 1600-3500kr; ⊙3-10pm; 🛜🗷🖩), a fabulous bistro-bar-cultural-centre. **Seyðisfjörður Tours** (📞785 4737; www.seydisfjordurtours. com; Norðurgata 6; ⊙Jun-mid-Sep) can rent you mountain bikes, take you on a guided walk or set you up on a scenic boat tour with a local fishing expert.

If the weather's good, the 27km drive from Egilsstaðir (take Rte 93, signed off Rte 1) is an absolute stunner, climbing to a high pass then descending along the waterfall-filled river Fjarðará.

Summer is the liveliest time to visit – but note that Wednesday nights are super-busy, as the ferry to Europe sails on Thursday mornings and rooms, meals and campsites in town are in hot demand. If you are taking the ferry, book your accommodation well ahead.

The full story about the French in Fáskrúðs-fjörður can be found at **Fosshotel Eastfjords** (📞470 4070; www.fosshotel. is; Hafnargata 11-14; d incl breakfast from 27,200kr; 🛜), a recent development inside the sensitively renovated former French hospital and other buildings from the era.

The Drive » The road traverses a valley before entering a 6km-long tunnel named Fáskrúðsfjarðargöng (that's quite a mouthful, even for locals). It emerges close to the head of Reyðarfjörður. Look right and you'll see the large Alcoa aluminium smelter, built here amid controversy in the early 2000s.

⑦ Reyðarfjörður

In the Prettiest Fjord pageant, Reyðarfjörður wouldn't be in the running to take home the crown. It's a relatively new settlement that only came into existence – as a trading port – in the 20th century. And if you feel the fabulous scenery is familiar? You may have seen Reyðarfjörður feature as the setting for British TV series *Fortitude*.

During WWII around 3000 Allied soldiers (10 times the local population) were based in Reyðarfjörður. The

Íslenska Stríðsárasafnið (http://stridsarasafn.fjardab yggd.is; Spítalakampu; adult/ child 1500kr/free; ⊙1-5pm Jun-Aug), or Icelandic Wartime Museum, details these strange few years. The building is surrounded by mines, Jeeps and aeroplane propellers, and holds other war relics. Photographs and tableaux provide a background to Iceland's wartime involvement.

The Drive » Fagridalur, an impressive river-lined valley, is a feature of the final stretch to Egilsstaðir; be on the lookout for reindeer here. (Reindeer were introduced from Norway in the 18th century and roam the mountains of the east.) Note,

too, the turnoff to Mjóifjörður, a narrow fjord to visit if you seek peace and isolation – the permanent population there is 14.

TRIP HIGHLIGHT

❽ Egilsstaðir (p97)

The town of Egilsstaðir isn't a ravishing beauty. It's the main regional transport hub, and a centre for local commerce, so its services are quite good (including quality accommodation and dining options). It's growing fast, but in a hotchpotch fashion. The best addition is the **Vök Baths** (www.facebook.com/vokbaths; Rte 925), a lakeside geothermal bathing area just out of town.

One of Egilsstaðir's saving graces is its proximity to **Lagarfljót**, Iceland's third-largest lake. Since Saga times, tales have been told of a monster living in its depths. The lake is a lovely stretch of water to circumnavigate by car. Rte 931, a mixture of sealed surfaces and gravel (gravel on the less-trafficked western shore), turns off Rte 95 about 10km south of Egilsstaðir and runs around the lake to Fellabær – a circuit of around 70km. Along the way are great diversions including forests, lakeside picnic areas, spectacular **Hengifoss** waterfall and the museum **Skriðuklaustur** (🕿471 2990; www.skriduklaustur.is; adult/child 1100kr/free; ⊙10am-6pm Jun-Aug, 11am-5pm May & Sep, noon-4pm Apr & Oct) and its superb **cafe** (lunch buffet adult/child 3490/1745kr) – go for the cake buffet.

North Iceland

Iceland's magnificent north is a nature-lover's dream. A wonderland of moon-like lava fields, belching mudpots, epic waterfalls, snowcapped peaks and whale-filled bays – this is Iceland at its best.

4

TRIP HIGHLIGHTS

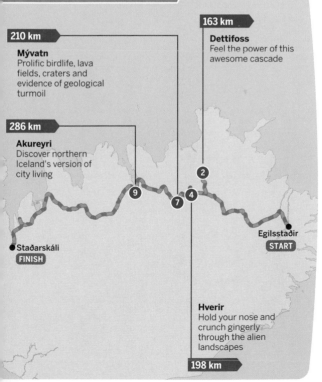

210 km

Mývatn
Prolific birdlife, lava fields, craters and evidence of geological turmoil

286 km

Akureyri
Discover northern Iceland's version of city living

163 km

Dettifoss
Feel the power of this awesome cascade

Staðarskáli
FINISH

Egilsstaðir
START

Hverir
Hold your nose and crunch gingerly through the alien landscapes

198 km

**4–5 DAYS
493KM / 306 MILES**

GREAT FOR...

BEST TIME TO GO
May to September for light and good weather; mid-November to March for winter activities.

ESSENTIAL PHOTO
Stand back! Thundering Dettifoss waterfall demonstrates nature at its most awesome.

BEST FOR RELAXATION
Soak in style at the Mývatn Nature Baths.

4 North Iceland

The region's top sights are variations on two themes: a grumbling, volcanically active Earth, and ice and water wending their way toward the ocean. Nature's masterpieces are everywhere you look. Take in little Akureyri, with its surprising moments of big-city living; windy pastures full of stout Viking horses; white-water rapids ready to deliver an adrenaline kick; unhyped and underpopulated ski fields; and lonely peninsulas stretching out toward the Arctic Circle.

❶ Möðrudalur

Leaving Egilsstaðir the Ring Road (Rte 1) tracks north, then turns south-west to follow the Jökulsá á Dal River for about 30km. From here, the Ring Road cuts a path inland across the stark highlands of the north-east interior. The barren, grey-toned landscape is dotted with low hills and small lakes caused by melting snowfields.

This area has always been a difficult place to eke out a living, and farms here are few and

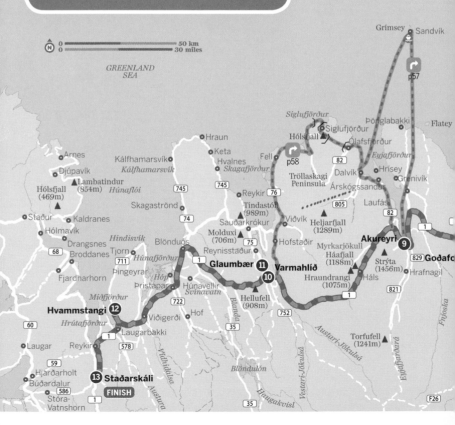

far between. Isolated Möðrudalur, an oasis in the desert, is the highest farm in Iceland at 469m. It's 8km south of the Ring Road on Rte 901, with the turnoff 104km west of Egilsstaðir. At Möðrudalur you'll find a popular mini-village, bustling in summer. **Fjalladýrð** (✆4711858; www.fjalladyrd.is; Rte 901; sites per person 1450kr, d with/without bathroom 35,000/15,900kr; 🛜) is the name of the tourist service, with camping, excellent accommodation and Jeep tours. Folks

simply passing through should stop for coffee and *kleina* (a traditional twisted doughnut), or try the farm-to-table dishes at **Fjallakaffi** (✆4711858; www.fjalladyrd.is; Rte 901; mains 2150-7490kr; ⏱7am-10pm May-Sep, shorter hours Oct-Apr; 🛜), the excellent restaurant here.

The Drive » Rejoin the Ring Road and press west through empty landscapes. After 26km you'll cross the bridge over the glacial river Jökulsá á Fjöllum, and 3km further is the sign indicating the 4WD-only Rte F88 to Askja in the highlands. Press on another 6km and

you'll reach the sealed road (Rte 862) to Dettifoss – take it, and drive 24km.

- - - - - - - - - - - - - - - -
> TRIP HIGHLIGHT

❷ Dettifoss

The power of nature in all its glory, Dettifoss is one of Iceland's most impressive waterfalls. The falls can be seen from either side of the canyon – Rte 862 links the Ring Road with the western bank, ending in a large car park and toilet facilities. From there, it's 1km to the falls, or a 2.5km loop via the dramatic,

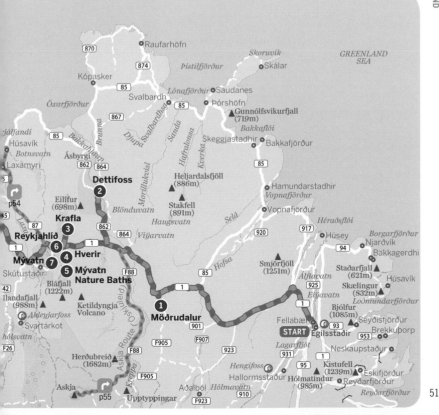

canyon-edge viewpoint, plus views of a smaller cataract, **Selfoss**.

Although it's 'only' 45m high and 100m wide, a massive 400 cubic metres of water thunders over Dettifoss's edge every second in summer, creating a spray plume that can be seen 1km away. With the greatest volume of any waterfall in Europe, this truly is nature at its most spectacular. On sunny days, brilliant double rainbows form above the churning milky-grey waters, and you'll have to jostle with the other visitors for the best views. Take care on the paths, made wet and slippery from the spray (and bring a raincoat).

The Drive » Waterfall cravings sated, head south to rejoin the Ring Road, then head

20km west and take Rte 863 to reach Krafla, 7km north.

- - - - - - - - - - - - - - - -

③ Krafla

Steaming vents and craters await at Krafla, an active volcanic region. Technically, Krafla is just an 818m-high mountain, but the name is now used for the entire area as well as a geothermal power station and the series of eruptions that created Iceland's most awesome lava field. There's a visitor centre at the power station if you're interested in learning about its workings. Beyond it is a great viewpoint over the landscapes.

Krafla's most impressive attraction is the **Leirhnjúkur** crater and its solfataras. In 1975, the Krafla Fires began with

a small lava eruption by Leirhnjúkur, and after nine years of on-and-off action Leirhnjúkur became the ominous-looking and sulphur-encrusted mud hole that tourists love today. The Earth's crust here is extremely thin and in places the ground is ferociously hot. A well-defined track leads northwest to Leirhnjúkur from the parking area; with all the volcanic activity, high temperatures, bubbling mudpots and steaming vents, it's best not to stray from the marked paths.

WINTER WONDERS

You're probably aware that the number of visitors to Iceland has skyrocketed in recent years. You may well be asking: what if there were a way to experience Iceland's awesome outdoors, but with smaller crowds? There is: visit in winter. For the Northern Lights, yes, but so much more.

Akureyri, the Tröllaskagi Peninsula and Mývatn are all winter wonderlands. Akureyri has winter festivals and easy access to Iceland's biggest ski field at Hlíðarfjall (p101). The Tröllaskagi Peninsula offers smaller ski fields plus great heliskiing (peak months: March and April). Mývatn has activities such as snowshoe and cross-country ski tours, snowmobiling on the frozen lake, and dog-sledding in the hills. Packages can be arranged that cover a variety of activities plus transfers and accommodation. A good tip is to travel from around February, when daylight hours are increasing.

Mývatn Nature Baths

The Drive ›› Once you're back on the Ring Road, it's barely a few metres to reach the next turn. Let the steam and the stench guide you.

TRIP HIGHLIGHT

4 Hverir

The magical, ochre-toned world of Hverir (also called Hverarönd) is a lunarlike landscape of mud cauldrons, steaming vents, radiant mineral deposits and piping fumaroles. Belching mudpots and the powerful stench of sulphur may not sound enticing, but Hverir's ethereal allure grips every passer-by.

Safe pathways through the features have been roped off; to avoid risk of serious injury and damage to the natural features, avoid any lighter-coloured soil and respect the ropes.

A walking trail loops from Hverir up **Námafjall** ridge behind the site. This 30-minute climb provides a grand vista over the steamy surroundings.

The Drive ›› The Ring Road climbs the pinky-orange Námafjall ridge that backs Hverir, and tumbles down its far side toward Mývatn. Pull over at the viewpoint on your left for impressive lake views.

You'll pass Bjarnarflag, an active geothermal area. Turn left at the turquoise pond (actually a toxic remnant of a diatomite plant).

5 Mývatn Nature Baths

Mývatn Nature Baths (Jarðböðin; ☎464 4411; www. myvatnnaturebaths.is; off Rte 1; adult/child 4700kr/free; ☙9am-midnight May–Sep, noon-10pm Oct-Apr), northern Iceland's answer to the Blue Lagoon, is 3km east of Reykjahlíð and the Mývatn lakeshore. Although it's smaller than its sparkling, magnetic southern counterpart, it's also cheaper and less

DETOUR: HÚSAVIK

Start: **6** **Reykjahlíð**

Húsavík, Iceland's whale-watching capital, has become a firm favourite on travellers' itineraries – and with its colourful houses, unique museums and stunning snowcapped peaks across Skjálfandi bay, it's easily the northeast's prettiest fishing town. It's 55km from Reykjahlíð via Rte 87. You can follow a different route back to the Ring Road if you wish – take Rte 85 and you'll rejoin the road just a kilometre or two west of Goðafoss waterfall.

Although there are other Iceland locales where you can do whale-watching tours (Reykjavík and Akureyri, for example), Húsavík has become Iceland's premier whale-watching destination, with up to 11 species coming here to feed in summer. The best time to see whales is between June and August. This is, of course, the height of tourist season, but you'll have a near-certain chance of seeing cetaceans.

Four whale-watching companies now operate from Húsavík harbour. Don't stress too much over picking an operator; prices are similar and services are comparable for the standard three-hour tour (guiding and warm overalls supplied, plus hot drinks and a pastry). When puffins are nesting (from roughly mid-April to mid-August), all companies offer tours that incorporate whale watching with a sail by the puffin-festooned island of Lundey. Where the differences are clear, however, is in the excursions that go beyond the standard. **North Sailing** (☑464 7272; www.northsailing.is; Garðarsbraut; 3hr tours adult/child 10,500/3500kr) offers one tour aboard an old schooner (hoisting sails when conditions are right), while **Gentle Giants** (☑464 1500; www.gentlegiants.is; Garðarsbraut; 3hr tours adult/child 10,400/4400kr) has both restored traditional vessels and high-speed rigid inflatable boats, plus tours taking in the serene island of Flatey.

You can wrap up your excursion at the new seawater baths, **GeoSea** (☑860 0202; www.geosea.is; Vitaslóð 1; adult/child 4300/1800kr; ☺9am-midnight May-Sep, noon-10pm Oct-Apr).

---

hyped (probably a good thing), and it's a gorgeous place to soak in the powder-blue, mineral-rich waters and enjoy the panorama. After a relaxing soak, try one of the two natural steam baths and/or a meal at the on-site cafeteria.

The Drive ≫ You'll barely get comfortable before you reach the next stop, 3km west of the Nature Baths.

6 Reykjahlíð (p98)

Reykjahlíð, on the northeastern lakeshore, is Mývatn region's main village and obvious base. There's little to it beyond a collection of guesthouses and hotels, a supermarket, a petrol station and an information centre. Accommodation here (and everywhere in the Mývatn area) is in strong demand, and the

prices reflect this. Book well ahead.

The well-informed Mývatnsstofa Visitor Centre (p100), by the supermarket, has good displays on the local geology, and the ranger can give advice on activities. Pick up a copy of the useful *Mývatn* map, which gives an overview of hiking trails in the area. All tours and buses leave from the car park here.

The Drive » Mývatn lake is encircled by a 36km sealed road (Rte 1 on the northern and western shores, and Rte 848 on the eastern and southern shoreline). Most sleeping and eating options are in Reykjahlíð or at Vógar, a hamlet about 2.5km south of Reykjahlíð. A further cluster of options lie along the southern lakeshore at Skútustaðir.

TRIP HIGHLIGHT

❼ Mývatn (p98)

Travelling clockwise around the lake from Reykjahlíð, geological wonders are thick on the ground, with the eastern shoreline holding the most appeal. The classic tephra ring **Hverfjall** (also called Hverfell) is an ancient and near-symmetrical crater, rising 452m and stretching 1040m across. It's an awe-inspiring landmark in Mývatn, and it's a relatively straightforward hike up to the top from a parking area at the ring's northwest.

Next is the giant jagged lava field at **Dimmuborgir** (Rte 884)

DETOUR: ASKJA & THE HIGHLANDS

Start: ❻ Reykjahlíð

Iceland's ravishing interior is so raw and remote that astronauts held astro-geological training exercises here before the 1969 lunar landings. This is true wilderness, with practically no services, accommodation or bridges (driving here involves fording large rivers; big 4WD vehicles are essential). Road access is only open a few months a year; the easiest way to visit is on a tour.

A number of operators run super-Jeep tours to Askja caldera and surrounds, from mid-June (when the roads open) until as late into September as weather permits. Day tours take around 12 hours and leave from Reykjahlíð. Recommended operators include **Saga Travel** (📞558 8888; www.sagatravel.is) and **Geo Travel** (📞864 7080; www.geotravel.is). Another operator, **Fjalladýrð** (📞4711858; www.fjalladyrd.is), runs from Möðrudalur.

The usual access road is Rte F88, which leaves the Ring Road 32km east of Mývatn; it's known as the Askja Route (Öskjuleið).

For much of the way the F88 is flat, following the western bank of the **Jökulsá á Fjöllum** glacier river, meandering across undulating tephra and winding through rough, tyre-abusing sections of the 4400-sq-km **Ódáðahraun** (Evil Deeds Lava Field).

After a long journey through the multihued lava fields and flood-smoothed plains, life explodes at the lovely oasis of **Herðubreiðarlindir**, at the foot of **Herðubreið** (1682m), the Icelanders' beloved 'Queen of the Mountains'. The route then wanders westward through dunes and lava flows to a parking area, where you leave your vehicle to walk 2.5km through the immense, 50-sq-km Askja caldera to its lake, **Öskjuvatn**.

Askja was created by a colossal explosion of tephra in 1875, and part of the collapsed magma chamber holds this sapphire-blue lake, the second-deepest in Iceland at 220m. Near the northeast corner is **Víti**, a tepid pool in a sienna crater where the milky-blue water (around 22°C) is popular for a swim and soak, although access involves a steep scramble.

(literally 'Dark Castles'). A series of nontaxing, colour-coded walking trails runs through the easily anthropomorphised landscape. There's a good cafe here, too.

The forested lava headland at **Höfði** (Rte 848) is one of the area's gentlest landscapes. Wildflowers, birch and spruce trees cover the bluffs, while the tiny islands and crystal-clear waters attract migratory birds. From footpaths along the shore you'll see small caves and stunning *klasar* (lava pillars).

The south side of the lake lures with its epic cache of pseudocraters. The **Skútustaðagígar** pseudocraters were formed when molten lava flowed into the lake, triggering a series of gas explosions. These dramatic green dimples then came into being when trapped subsurface water boiled and popped, forming small scoria cones and craters.

Western Mývatn offers some of the best **birdwatching** in Iceland, with more than 115 species recorded in the area – including 28 species of ducks. For good birdwatching background, swing by the excellent

Sigurgeir's Bird Museum

(Fuglasafn Sigurgeirs; ☎464 4477; www.fuglasafn.is; off Rte 1, Ytri-Neslönd farm; adult/child 1500/800kr; ⏱noon–5pm mid-May–Oct, reduced hours rest of year).

The Drive ❯❯ The Ring Road continues west from the lake region. About 33km from Mývatn's southwest corner toward Akureyri you'll happen across heavenly, horseshoe-shaped Goðafoss.

- - - - - - - - - - - - - - - - - -

❽ Goðafoss

Goðafoss (Waterfall of the Gods) rips straight through the Bárðardalur lava field along the Ring Road, and it's a magnet that pulls most drivers off the road for a closer look. Although smaller and less powerful than some of Iceland's other chutes, it's definitely one of the most beautiful. There are two car parks – one on the Ring Road, the other down the road beside the petrol station. Take the path behind the falls for a less crowded viewpoint.

The falls play an important part in Icelandic history. At the Alþingi (National Assembly) in the year 1000, the *lögsögumaður* (law speaker), Þorgeir, was forced to make a decision on Iceland's religion. After 24 hours of meditation, he declared the country a Christian nation. On his way home he passed the waterfall near his farm, and tossed in his pagan

---

THE LOWDOWN ON MÝVATN

Mývatn (pronounced *mee*-vaht) is the calm, shallow lake at the heart of a volatile volcanic area that sits squarely on the Mid-Atlantic Ridge. Nature's violent masterpieces are everywhere: crazy-coloured mudpots, huge craters and jagged lava fields. Once you've had your fill of geology gone wild, mellow out with walks, bicycle rides and top-notch birdwatching (geese, golden plovers, swans and ducks) – and plenty of soaks at the nature baths.

Most of the points of interest are linked by the lake's looping road. The area (plus the awesome natural highlights east of Reykjahlíð at Hverir and Krafla) can be explored in a full and busy day, but two days is better, and if you want to hike and explore more distant mountains and lava fields (or take a day tour to Askja in the highlands), allow at least three days.

The downside to Mývatn (its name translates as 'Midge Lake') are the dense midge clouds that appear during summer, with tiny insects intent on flying up your nose. You may want to wear a head net (which you can buy at the supermarket in Reykjahlíð, and elsewhere) – and pray for a good wind, which seems to curtail their activity.

carvings of the Norse gods, thus bestowing the falls' present name.

The Drive » It's a scenic drive west to Eyjafjörður and Akureyri. Note that a 7.5km-long tunnel was recently built on Eyjafjörður's eastern side, which shortens the Ring Road journey by about 16km. Drivers can now avoid the mountain pass Víkurskarð, which is often blocked by winter snows.

`TRIP HIGHLIGHT`

❾ Akureyri (p100)

Akureyri stands strong as Iceland's second city, but a Melbourne, Manchester or Montreal it is not. And how could it be? There are only 18,000 residents! Despite its diminutive size, you can expect cool cafes, quality restaurants and something of a late-night bustle – a far cry from other towns in rural Iceland. With its scenic setting, relaxed attitude and extensive accommodation choices, it's a natural base for exploring the north.

Akureyri nestles at the head of Eyjafjörður, Iceland's longest (60km) fjord, at the base of snowcapped peaks. In summer, well-tended gardens belie the location, just a stone's throw from the Arctic Circle. Lively winter festivals and some of Iceland's best skiing provide plenty of off-peak (and off-piste) appeal. It's a place geared for small pleasures and gentle

DETOUR: GRÍMSEY

Start: ❾ Akureyri

Best known as Iceland's only true piece of the Arctic Circle, the remote island of Grímsey, 40km from the mainland, is a tranquil little place where birds outnumber people by about 10,000 to one. The island is small (5 sq km, with a year-round population of 61), but the welcome is big.

Grímsey's appeal to many lies in what it represents. Tourists flock here to snap up their 'I visited the Arctic Circle' certificate and appreciate its windswept setting. Though the Arctic Circle is shown on maps at a fixed 66.5°, it actually moves with the wobble of the Earth's tilt (2.4° every 40,000 years). As of 2017, a 7980kg concrete sphere marks the actual spot on the island, currently about a 45-minute hike north of the airstrip. So, unless you are a runner, the best way to ensure you actually get to the real Arctic Circle is by coming by boat (longer layover) or staying the night – two small guesthouses offer accommodation.

With time to appreciate the windswept setting, hike along scenic coastal cliffs and dramatic basalt formations; they are a popular home for dozens of species of seabirds, including loads of puffins, plus the kamikaze Arctic tern.

There are several options for reaching Grímsey. Year-round, there are flights and ferries a few times a week. Flights depart from Akureyri; journey time is half an hour. Ferries run from Dalvík, 43km north of Akureyri; sailing time is three hours one way. Air and boat tours are an option in summer months; Akureyri is the hub for these. For more info, see www.grimsey.is.

strolling. Stop at the botanic gardens, **Lysti-garðurinn** (☏462 7487; www.lystigardur.akureyri.is; Eyrarlandsholt; ☺8am-10pm, from 9am Sat & Sun Jun-Sep), and admire **Akurey-rarkirkja** (☏462 7700; www.akureyrarkirkja.is; Eyrarlands-vegur; ☺generally 10am-4pm

Mon-Fri), the landmark church designed by the same architect responsible for Reykjavík's Hall-grímskirkja. Take it easy at the local **swimming pool** (☏461 4455; www.visitakureyri.is; Þingvallastræti 21; adult/child 950/250kr; ☺6.45am-9pm Mon-Fri,

DETOUR: TRÖLLASKAGI

Start: 9 Akureyri

Tröllaskagi (Troll Peninsula) rests its mountainous bulk between the scenic fjords of Skagafjörður and Eyjafjörður. Here, the craggy peaks, deep valleys and gushing rivers are more reminiscent of the Westfjords than the gentle hills that roll through most of North Iceland. Tunnels now link the northern Tröllaskagi townships of Siglufjörður and Ólafsfjörður, once dead-end towns that saw little tourist traffic.

The journey from Akureyri to Varmahlíð along the Ring Road (Rte 1) measures 95 very scenic kilometres, but if you have some time up your sleeve and a penchant for getting off the beaten track, the 186km journey between those two towns following the Tröllaskagi coastline (Rtes 82 and 76) conjures up some magical scenery, dramatic tunnels, and plenty of excuses to pull over and explore. Worthy pit stops include ferries to offshore islands Grímsey and Hrísey, whale-watching tours on Eyjafjörður, a **microbrewery** (Kaldi Beer; ☑466 2505; www.bruggsmidjan.is; Öldugata 22, Árskógssandur; tour 2000kr; ☺tours by appointment) and **beer baths** (☑414 2828; www.bjorbodin.is; Ægisgata 31, Árskógssandur; beer bath 7900kr; ☺noon-8pm, 11am-9pm Fri & Sat), ski fields, Siglufjörður's colourful harbour front and outstanding **herring museum** (Síldarminjasafnið; ☑467 1604; www.sild.is; Snorragata 10; adult/child 1800kr/free; ☺10am-6pm Jun-Aug, 1-5pm May & Sep, by appointment rest of year), and Hofsós' dreamy fjord-side **swimming pool** (Sundlaugin á Hofsósi; ☑455 6070; www.facebook.com/sundlauginhofsosi; Suðurbraut; adult/child 900/300kr; ☺7am-9pm Jun-Aug, shorter hours Sep-May).

8am-9pm Sat, 8am-7.30pm Sun; 🛈), and indulge in some dining, drinking and shopping along Hafnarstræti. If there's a live show at **Græni Hatturinn** (☑461 4646; http://graenihatturinn.is; Hafnarstræti 96), snap up a ticket – this intimate venue is the best place in town to see live music (and one of the best in the country).

There are also plenty of ways to get out among the surrounding landscapes – from horse rides to hikes, whale-watching cruises to golf under the midnight sun. Visit www.visitakureyri.is for more

info, and consider joining a tour with the likes of Saga Travel (p98).

The Drive » The highlight of the 93km Ring Road stretch between Akureyri and Varmahlíð is Öxnadalur, a narrow, 30km-long valley. Stunning peaks and thin pinnacles of rock flank the mountain pass.

- - - - - - - - - - - - - - -

10 Varmahlíð (p103)

This Ring Road service centre is slightly more than a road junction and yet not quite a town, and it's a great spot for whitewater rafting and horse riding. Most activity operators have a base along

the sealed Rte 752, just south of the township's large N1 petrol station complex.

The northwest region is horse country, and companies in and around Varmahlíð offer menus of shorter rides (one to two hours) for beginners, plus longer day outings in wild landscapes. A few companies run weeklong expeditions into the highlands. **Hestasport** (☑453 8383; www.riding.is) is one of Iceland's most respected riding outfits, and runs a smart complex of cottages in town. The lovely farm

Lýtingsstaðir (☏453 8064; www.lythorse.com; Rte 752; 1/2hr horse ride 6000/9000kr) has a great program of short and long rides, plus accommodation.

Varmahlíð also gives access to northern Iceland's best white-water rafting. **Bakkaflöt** (☏453 8245; www.bakkaflot.com) and **Viking Rafting** (☏823 8300; www.vikingrafting.com) lead trips on the high-octane Austari-Jökulsá (East Glacial River; Class 4+ rapids) and the more placid, family-friendly Vestari-Jökulsá (West Glacial River; Class 2+ rapids).

The Drive » Following Rte 75 north from Varmahlíð leads to the 18th-century turf-farm museum at Glaumbær. It's the best museum of its type in northern Iceland and worth the easy 8km detour off the Ring Road.

⓫ Glaumbær

The traditional Icelandic turf farm was a complex of small separate buildings, connected by a central passageway. At the photogenic **Glaumbær** (www.glaumbaer.is; Rte 75; adult/child 1700kr/free; ☉9am-6pm mid-May–mid-Sep, 10am-4pm Mon-Fri early May & mid-Sep–mid-Oct) museum you can see this style of construction, with some building compartments stuffed full of period furniture,

equipment and utensils. It gives a fascinating insight into the cramped living conditions of the era.

Also on the site are two 19th-century houses – one is home to **Áskaffi**, an impossibly quaint tearoom with old-world atmosphere and doll's-house dishware.

The Drive » Return to Varmahlíð and reconnect with the Ring Road, which tracks west then northwest through Langidalur (Long Valley) to the service town of Blönduós. From Blönduós, the road heads southwest through windswept landscapes and past fields of horses; take the turn-off at Rte 72, which leads 6km to the town of Hvammstangi.

⓬ Hvammstangi (p104)

Sweet, slow-paced Hvammstangi builds its appeal around the local seal colonies. Visitors come to take a seal-watching cruise, go horse riding in the area, or drive the scenic loop around the Vatnsnes Peninsula. The town's prime attraction is the **Icelandic Seal Centre** (☏451 2345; www.selasetur.is; Strandgata 1; adult/child 1100kr/free; ☉9am-7pm Jun-Aug, to 4pm May & Sep, noon-3pm Mon-Fri Apr-Oct) on the harbourfront, where you can learn about the history and conservation of the area's seals.

With time up your sleeve, consider taking a couple of hours to drive around the starkly beautiful **Vatnsnes Peninsula**. It's about 82km in total, from the Ring Road to Hvammstangi and around the peninsula on Rte 711, a gravel road (drive slowly).

On Vatnsnes' west coast, stop by storied farm **Illugastaðir**. A 10-minute walk through bird-filled fields leads from the car park to a popular site for sunbaking seals. On the east coast, stop at the photogenic 15m-high sea stack called **Hvítserkur**, which looks like a huge stone beast drinking from the water. Nearby, a walking path takes you down to a scenic black-sand beach and views to a large seal haul-out site.

The Drive » Rejoin the Ring Road; from Hvammstangi it's about 35km to the next stop.

⓭ Staðarskáli

The inlet of little Hrútafjörður marks the divide between Northwest Iceland and the West. As you follow the Ring Road, you'll encounter Staðarskáli. No more than a road junction with a big, busy N1 petrol station and cafeteria, Staðarskáli acts as a popular leg-stretching spot for motorists.

West Iceland

5

West Iceland offers everything from windswept beaches and historic villages to awe-inspiring volcanic and glacial terrain in one neat little package.

TRIP HIGHLIGHTS

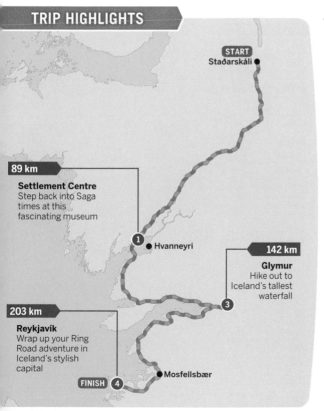

START
Staðarskáli

89 km

Settlement Centre
Step back into Saga times at this fascinating museum

1 Hvanneyri

142 km

Glymur
Hike out to Iceland's tallest waterfall

3

203 km

Reykjavík
Wrap up your Ring Road adventure in Iceland's stylish capital

FINISH **4**

● Mosfellsbær

1–2 DAYS
203KM / 126 MILES

GREAT FOR...

BEST TIME TO GO
June to August brings the best weather and the most activities.

ESSENTIAL PHOTO

Light changing across iconic seaside mountain, Kirkjufell.

BEST FOR HISTORY & CULTURE
Discover the Saga sites of famous *Egil's Saga* in zippy Borgarnes.

Borgarnes Home of Iceland's earliest settlers (p62)

61

5 West Iceland

Geographically close to Reykjavík yet far, far away in sentiment, West Iceland (known as Vesturland) is a splendid blend of Iceland's offerings. Two of the best-known sagas, *Egil's Saga* and *Laxdæla Saga*, took place along the region's brooding waters, marked today by haunting cairns and an exceptional museum in lively Borgarnes. The long arm of Snæfellsnes Peninsula, inland lava tubes and remote highland glaciers are added enticements.

TRIP HIGHLIGHT

❶ Borgarnes (p104)

Follow the Ring Road from Staðarskáli's petrol station 89km south to Borgarnes. You'll pass through rolling plains along the Norðurá river valley, with buttes rising in the distance; on clear days, you can see all the way to the ice cap at Langjökull. Around Hraunsnef you'll enter a rich lava-field zone with day hikes, and finally pass through light for-

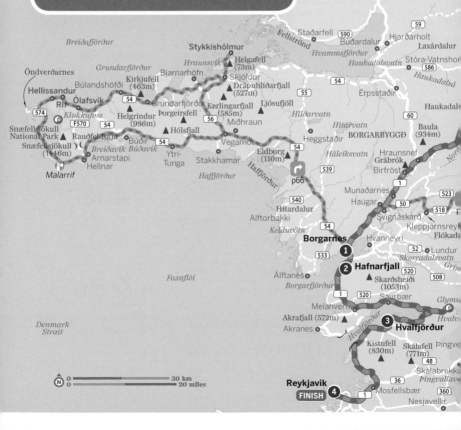

est and summer-house encampments around Munaðarnes, before descending into the river deltas and fjord zone around Borgarnes.

Buzzy Borgarnes, on a scenic promontory along the broad waters of **Borgarfjörður**, was the landing zone for several of Iceland's famous first settlers. Housed in an imaginatively restored warehouse by the harbour, the fascinating **Settlement Centre** (Landnámssetur Íslands; ☎437 1600; www.settlementcentre. is; Brákarbraut 13-15; adult/

child 2500kr/free; ☺10am-9pm) offers insights into the history of Icelandic settlement and brings alive the story of one of its most famous settlers, poet-warrior Egil Skallagrímsson (the man behind *Egil's Saga*). The centre has also placed cairns throughout town marking key sites from *Egil's Saga*.

Borg á Mýrum (Rock in the Marshes), just northwest of Borgarnes on Rte 54, is where Skallagrímur Kveldúlfsson, Egil's father, made his farm at Settlement. It was named for the large rock *(borg)* behind the farmstead. You can walk up to the **cairn** for super views. The small **cemetery** includes an ancient rune-inscribed gravestone. Ásmundur Sveinsson's **sculpture** represents Egil mourning the death of his sons and his rejuvenation in poetry.

To unwind after your historical studies, visit Borgarnes' excellent fjord-side **geothermal pool** (www.borgarbyggd. is; Þorsteinsgata; adult/child 900/300kr; ☺6am-10pm Mon-Fri, 9am-6pm Sat & Sun).

The Drive » Zip a mere 3.5km south on the Ring Road, crossing Borgarnes' long sweep of causeway to reach the trailhead for Hafnarfjall, the mountain rising precipitously from the water's edge south of the city.

---

❷ Hafnarfjall

The dramatically sheer mountain **Hafnarfjall** (844m) rises south across the fjord from Borgarnes. You can climb it along a 7km path from the trailhead on Rte 1, near the southern base of the causeway into Borgarnes. Be careful of slippery scree cliffs once you ascend. If you make it all the way up the steep slopes, you'll get sweeping views from the top.

For the more domestically inclined, find your way to off-the-beaten-path village Hvanneyri, 12km northeast of Hafnarfjall, to visit **Ullarselið** (☎437 0077; www.ull.is; ☺11am-5pm Jun-Aug, 1-5pm Thu-Sat Sep-May), a fantastic wool centre that's part of the Agricultural Museum of Iceland. Handmade sweaters, scarves, hats and blankets share space with skeins of beautiful hand-spun yarn, and interesting bone and shell buttons. Plus there are needles and patterns to get you started. Look out for local Borgarfjörður designs featuring geese, ptarmigan or salmon.

The Drive » This drive will skirt you around the base of Hafnarfjall and 28km along inland mountains, with glistening ocean just to the west. Turn east at Rte 47 to reach and

follow Hvalfjörður's edge. Those in a hurry to reach Reykjavík can skip the fjord by continuing on the Ring Road straight through the 5.7km-long tunnel beneath the fjord.

TRIP HIGHLIGHT

❸ Hvalfjörður

This sparkling fjord is about 30km long, and

lies between Akranes and Mosfellsbær. The lush area feels quite pastoral despite being a mere 30-minute drive from the capital. It's the site of a whaling station (*hvalur* means whale in Icelandic) and an aluminium smelting plant (not as unsightly as it sounds!). In-

terestingly, during WWII the fjord contained a submarine station; over 20,000 American and British soldiers passed through. Learn more at **War & Peace Museum** (Hernámssetrið; ☏433 8877; www.warandpeace.is; Hlaðir, Hvalfjarðarströnd; adult/child 1250kr/free; ☉1-5pm Wed-Fri,

DETOUR: UPPER BORGARBYGGÐ

Start: ❶ Borgarnes

Inland from Borgarnes, up river-twined valleys skirted by Rte 50 in the Upper Borgarbyggð area, you'll find fertile farms with deep history leading to stone-strewn lava tubes and highlands, the gateway to ice caps beyond. The following 130km route can be done in one long day; overnight in Húsafell to include glacier or lava-tube activities.

Europe's biggest hot spring, **Deildartunguhver**, lies about 5km west of Reykholt, just off Rte 50. Look for billowing clouds of steam rising from scalding water bubbling from the ground (180L per second and 100°C). New spa **Krauma** offers sleek hot pools, a cold pool and two steam rooms.

The interesting medieval study centre **Snorrastofa** (☏433 8000; www.snorrastofa.is; 1200kr; ☉10am-6pm Apr-Sep, to 5pm Mon-Fri Oct-Mar) in Reykholt is devoted to celebrated poet, historian and statesman Snorri Sturluson, and is built on his old farm, where he was brutally slain.

Next, stop **Hraunfossar** – the name of this spectacular waterfall translates to Lava Field Waterfall because the crystalline water streams out from below surrounding lava fields. Find the turnout on the north side of Rte 518, 6.5km west of Húsafell.

Tucked into an emerald, river-crossed valley, with the river Kaldá on one side and a dramatic lava field on the other, **Húsafell** is an encampment of summer cottages, and its chic **hotel** (☏435 1551; www.hotelhusafell.com; Rte 518; d incl breakfast from 34,200kr; P🛜) is a popular retreat for Reykjavikers and a top spot to dine.

Langjökull ice cap is the second-largest glacier in Iceland, and the closest major glacier to Reykjavík. Do not attempt to drive up onto the glacier yourself. Tours depart from Húsafell (or Reykjavík): **Into the Glacier** (Langjökull Ice Cave; ☏578 2550; www.intotheglacier.is) ice cave is a major tourist attraction and **Mountaineers of Iceland** (☏580 9900; www.mountaineers.is) offers snowmobiling.

The largest lava tube in Iceland, 1100-year-old, 1.5km-long **Viðgelmir** (☏783 3600; www.thecave.is; tour per adult/child from 6500kr/free) is located on private property near farmstead Fljótstunga. It sparkles with ever-changing rock formations and has a stable walkway on which tours are conducted.

Hraunfossar waterfall

from 10am Sat & Sun late May-Aug).

The **church** (Hallgrímskirkja í Saurbæ; Rte 47) at Saurbær farmstead features beautiful stained-glass work by Gerður Helgadóttir. It's named Hallgrímskirkja (the same name as Reykjavík's famous church) for Reverend Hallgrímur Pétursson, who served here from 1651 to 1669. He composed Iceland's most popular religious work, *Passion Hymns.*

Glymur, Iceland's highest waterfall at 198m (though some allege that a taller one was found in 2010) lies at the head of Hvalfjörður. Reach the trailhead by following the turn-off to Botnsdalur. From the end of the bumpy road, you must then hike a couple of hours on rough trails to reach the cascades. Note that a log is placed to bridge a river along the way only in summer.

On the southern side of Hvalfjörður dramatic **Mt Esja** (914m) is a great spot for wilderness hiking. The most popular trail begins at Esjustofa Hiking Center (with a cafe), just north of Mosfellsbær. Most people hike 2.8km to the viewpoint at Steinn. It gets much more technical after that.

The Drive » From the southern shore of Hvalfjörður, rejoin the Ring Road and travel 28km into Reykjavík. As you leave raw mountains and shining shores behind, you'll start to see the profile of Hallgrímskirkja rising on Reykjavík's peninsula. To head into the centre, leave the Ring Road at Rte 49 and continue due west.

TRIP HIGHLIGHT

❹ Reykjavík (p70)

The world's most northerly capital combines colourful buildings, creative people, eye-popping design, wild nightlife and a capricious soul to devastating effect. In many ways Reykjavík is strikingly cosmopolitan for its size. After all, it's merely a town by international standards, and yet it's loaded with excellent museums, captivating art, rich culinary choices, and offbeat cafes and bars. Add a backdrop of snow-topped mountains, churning seas and crystal-clear air, and you, like many visitors, may fall helplessly in love, returning home already saving to come back.

Start with a walk around the Old Reykjavík quarter (p70) near Tjörnin (p71), then peruse the city's best museums, such as the impressive National Museum (p70), Reykjavík Art Museum (p71) or The Settlement Exhibition (p70). Wander up arty **Skólavörðustígur** to the immense Hallgrímskirkja (p72). For a perfect view, take the elevator up the tower, then circle down to stroll **Laugavegur**, the main shopping drag.

Many of the more lively restaurants turn into party hang-outs

DETOUR: SNÆFELLSNES PENINSULA

Start: ❶ Borgarnes

Sparkling fjords, dramatic volcanic peaks, sheer sea cliffs, sweeping golden beaches and crunchy lava flows make up the diverse and fascinating landscape of the 100km-long Snæfellsnes Peninsula. The area is crowned by the glistening ice cap Snæfellsjökull, immortalised in Jules Verne's *Journey to the Centre of the Earth*. It offers a cross-section of the best Iceland has to offer in a very compact region.

You'll circle the peninsula over the course of one long day, or two leisurely days, on Rte 54, starting at **Stykkishólmur**, on the populated northern coast. It is the region's largest town and super quaint to boot. Moving west along the northern coast, you'll pass smaller townships perfect for joining a whale- or puffin-viewing tour. Or head out to the windswept point at **Öndverðarnes** for lighthouses and occasional sightings of whales offshore. As you make this westerly drive, look for **Kirkjufell** near the town of **Grundarfjörður**; it's an iconic mountain that appears often on posters or in movies, and is backed by vibrant cascades.

On the western part of the peninsula, **Snæfellsjökull National Park** (☎436 6860; www.snaefellsjokull.is) encompasses not only its eponymous glacier, but bird sanctuaries, lava fields and other volcanic craters. You'll find the park **visitor centre** (☎591 2000, 436 6888; ◔10am-5pm late Apr-Oct, 11am-4pm Mon-Fri rest of year; ☎) at the lighthouse at **Malarrif**; there's excellent online maps of the area as well. The quiet southern coast is lined with remote beaches and has several good horse farms along the verdant meadows that lie beneath towering inland crags. There is a scenic coastal walk between the hamlets of **Hellnar** and **Arnarstapi**.

Follow Rte 54 back inland and then south to where it joins the Ring Road just to the north of Borgarnes.

Stykkishólmur

at night. Eat well – the options seem endless these days and can fit any budget or palate – then enjoy people-watching and drinks as you join Reykjavík's notorious pub-crawl (*djammið* in Icelandic).

After a late night out, get a big Icelandic brunch and visit Harpa (p72), the iconic concert hall, and then the Old Harbour (p71). You can visit the harbour's museums, such as the Reykjavík Maritime Museum (p71), Saga Museum (p71) or Whales of Iceland (p71), tour a chocolate factory at Omnom Chocolate (p71), or head out on a whale-watching tour (p76).

Destinations

Reykjavík (p70)

Iceland's addictive capital is where everything's at, and has a heady blend of fresh air, stylish design, artfully hip cafes and bars, fabulous and unusual museums plus a thriving restaurant scene.

The Golden Circle (p88)

In striking distance of the capital, this circuit comprises some standout natural attractions, including the world's oldest parliament, shifting tectonic plates, the original geyser and a stunning waterfall.

Akureyri (p100)

Iceland's second city packs a punch for a diminutive town and is worth getting to know. There's a quality restaurant and art scene, and the only decent nightlife beyond Reykjavík.

Reykjavík

A vibrant small city with a lot of soul, Reykjavík is a cultural hub of innovative, offbeat art, music and design; its crisp clear air also thrums with culinary creativity and a rampant bar scene.

History

Ingólfur Arnarson, a Norwegian fugitive, became the first official Icelander in AD 871, and Reykjavík was just a simple collection of farm buildings for centuries. It expanded in the 1750s when local sheriff Skúli Magnússon, the 'Father of Reykjavík', created weaving, tanning and wool-dyeing factories – the foundations of the city – to bypass a Danish monopoly. Today, with continuously rising visitor numbers and endlessly innovative locals, central Reykjavík has exploded with renewed growth.

◎ Sights

The compact city centre contains most of Reykjavík's attractions, which range from interesting walking and shopping streets to excellent museums and picturesque promenades.

◎ Old Reykjavík

★**Old Reykjavík**   AREA
(Map p78) With a series of sights and interesting historic buildings, the area dubbed Old Reykjavík is the heart of the capital, and the focal point of many historic walking tours. The area is anchored by Tjörnin, the city-centre lake, and sitting between it and Austurvöllur park to the north are the Raðhús (city hall) and Alþingi (Parliament).

★**National Museum**   MUSEUM
(Map p78; Þjóðminjasafn Íslands; ☑ 530 2200; www.nationalmuseum.is; Suðurgata 41; adult/child 2000kr/free; ◎ 10am-5pm daily May–mid-Sep, closed Mon mid-Sep–Apr; ⬚ 1, 3, 6, 12, 14) Artifacts from settlement to the modern age fill the creative display spaces of Iceland's superb National Museum. Exhibits give an excellent overview of Iceland's history and culture, and the free smartphone audio guide adds a wealth of detail. The strongest section describes the Settlement Era – including the rule of the chieftans and the introduction of Christianity – and features swords, drinking horns, silver hoards and a powerful bronze figure of Thor. The priceless 13th-century Valþjófsstaðir church door is carved with the story of a knight, his faithful lion and a passel of dragons.

Settlement Exhibition   MUSEUM
(Map p78; Landnámssýningin; ☑ 411 6370; www.reykjavikmuseum.is; Aðalstræti 16; adult/child 1650kr/free; ◎ 9am-6pm) This fascinating archaeological ruin-museum is based around a 10th-century Viking longhouse unearthed here from 2001 to 2002 and other settlement-era finds from central Reykjavík. It imaginatively combines technological wizardry and archaeology to give a glimpse into early Icelandic life. Don't miss the fragment of **boundary wall** at the back of the museum that is older still (and the oldest human-made structure in Reykjavík). Among the captivating high-tech displays, a wraparound panorama shows how things would have looked at the time of the longhouse.

Tjörnin
LAKE

(Map p78) The placid lake at the centre of the city is sometimes called the Pond. It echoes with the honks and squawks of more than 40 species of visiting birds, including swans, geese and Arctic terns; feeding the ducks is a popular pastime for under-fives. Pretty sculpture-dotted parks like Hljómskálagarður FREE line the southern shores, and their paths are much used by cyclists and joggers. In winter hardy souls strap on ice skates and the lake transforms into an outdoor rink.

◎ Old Harbour

★ Old Harbour
AREA

(Map p78; Geirsgata; 🚌1, 3, 6, 11, 12, 13, 14) Largely a service harbour until recently, the Old Harbour and the neighbouring Grandi area have blossomed into tourist hot spots, with key art galleries, several museums, volcano and Northern Lights films, and excellent restaurants. Whale-watching and puffin-viewing trips depart from the pier. Photo ops abound with views of fishing boats, the Harpa concert hall and snowcapped mountains beyond. On the western edge of the harbour, the Grandi area, named after the fish factory there, is burgeoning with eateries and shops.

★ Omnom Chocolate
FACTORY

(Map p74; ☑519 5959; www.omnomchocolate.com; Hólmaslóð 4, Grandi; adult/child 3000/1500kr; ◎11am-6pm Mon-Fri, noon-4pm Sat) Reserve ahead for a tour (2pm Monday to Friday) at this full-service chocolate factory where you'll see how cocoa beans are transformed into high-end scrumptious delights. The shop sells its stylish bars (packaged with specially designed labels), which come in myriad sophisticated flavours.

Kling & Bang
GALLERY

(Map p78; ☑554 20 03; http://this.is/klingand bang; Grandagarður 20, Marshall Húsið, Grandi; ◎noon-6pm Wed & Fri-Sun, to 9pm Thu; 🚌14) FREE This perennially cutting-edge artist-run exhibition space is a favourite with locals, and now has an expanded gallery in the renovated Marshall House in the Grandi area beside the Old Harbour.

Saga Museum
MUSEUM

(Map p78; ☑7511 1517; www.sagamuseum.is; Grandagarður 2; adult/child 2200/800kr; ◎10am-6pm; 🚌14) The endearingly bloodthirsty Saga Museum is where Icelandic history is brought to life by eerie silicon models and a multi-language soundtrack featuring the

REYKJAVÍK ART MUSEUM

The excellent **Reykjavík Art Museum** (Listasafn Reykjavíkur; www.artmuseum. is; adult/child 1650kr/free; 🚇) is split over three superbly curated sites: the large, modern downtown **Hafnarhús** (Map p78; ☑411 6400; Tryggvagata 17; ◎10am-5pm, to 10pm Thu; 🚌1, 3, 6, 11, 12, 13, 14), focusing on contemporary art; **Kjarvalsstaðir** (Map p74; ☑411 6420; Flókagata 24, Miklatún Park; ◎10am-5pm; 🚇), in a park just east of Snorrabraut which displays rotating exhibits of modern art; and **Ásmundarsafn** (Map p74; Ásmundur Sveinsson Museum; ☑411 6430; Sigtún; ◎10am-5pm May-Sep, 1-5pm Oct-Apr; 🚇; 🚌2, 4, 14, 15, 17, 19), a peaceful haven near Laugardalur for viewing sculptures by Ásmundur Sveinsson. One ticket (valid for 24 hours) gains entry to all three sites.

thud of axes and hair-raising screams. Don't be surprised if you see some of the characters wandering around town, as moulds were taken from Reykjavík residents (the owner's daughters are the Irish princess and the little slave gnawing at a fish).

Aurora Reykjavík
MUSEUM

(Map p78; Northern Lights Centre; ☑780 4500; www.aurorareykjavik.is; Grandagarður 2; adult/child 1600/1000kr; ◎9am-9pm; 🚌14) Learn about the classical tales explaining the Northern Lights, and the scientific explanation, then watch a 35-minute surround-sound panoramic high-definition re-creation of Icelandic auroras.

Reykjavík Maritime Museum
MUSEUM

(Map p78; Sjóminjasafnið í Reykjavík; ☑411 6300; www.maritimemuseum.is; Grandagarður 8; adult/child 1650kr/free; Óðinn & museum 2600kr; ◎10am-5pm, Óðinn tours at 11am, 1pm, 2pm & 3pm; 🚻; 🚌14) The crucial role fishing plays in Iceland's economy is celebrated through the imaginative displays in this former fish-freezing plant. The new exhibition **Fish & Folk** evokes 150 years of the industry, using artefacts, sepia photos and interactive games to chart a course from the row boats of the late 1800s to the trawlers of the 21st century. Make time for one of the daily guided tours of the former coastguard ship Óðinn (1300kr).

Whales of Iceland
MUSEUM

(Map p78; ☑571 0077; www.whalesoficeland.is; Fiskislóð 23; adult/child 2900/1500kr; ◎10am-5pm; 🚇; 🚌14) Ever strolled beneath a blue whale?

This museum houses full-sized models of the 23 species of whale found off Iceland's coast. The largest museum of this type in Europe, it also displays models of whale skeletons, and has good audio guides and multimedia screens to explain what you're seeing. There's a cafe and gift shop too. Look out for online ticket discounts and family tickets (5800kr).

⊙ Laugavegur & Skólavörðustígur

★Hallgrímskirkja   CHURCH

(Map p78; ☑510 1000; www.hallgrimskirkja.is; Skólavör-ðustígur; tower adult/child 1000/100kr; ⊙9am-9pm May-Sep, to 5pm Oct-Apr) Reykjavík's immense white-concrete church (1945–86), star of a thousand postcards, dominates the skyline and is visible from up to 20km away. An elevator trip up the 74.5m-high tower reveals an unmissable view of the city. In contrast to the high drama outside, the Lutheran church's interior is quite plain. The most eye-catching feature is the vast 5275-pipe organ installed in 1992. The church's size and radical design caused controversy, and its architect, Guðjón Samúelsson (1887–1950), never saw its completion.

The columns on either side of the tower represent volcanic basalt, part of Samúelsson's desire to create a national architectural style. At the front, gazing proudly into the distance, is a statue of the Viking Leifur Eiríksson, the first European to discover America. Designed by Alexander Stirling Calder (1870–1945), it was a present from the US on the 1000th anniversary of the Alþingi (Parliament) in 1930.

From mid-June to late August, hear half-hour **choir concerts** (www.scholacantorum. is; 2500kr) at noon on Wednesday and **organ recitals** (www.listvinafelag.is) at noon on Thursday and Saturday (2000kr), and for one hour at 5pm on Sunday (2500kr). Services are held on Sunday at 11am, with a small service Wednesday at 8am. There is an English service the last Sunday of the month at 2pm.

★Harpa   ARTS CENTRE

(Map p78; ☑box office 528 5050; www.harpa. is; Austurbakki 2; ⊙8am-midnight, box office noon-6pm; ⊛) With its ever-changing facets glistening on the water's edge, Reykjavík's sparkling Harpa concert hall and cultural centre is a beauty to behold. In addition to a season of top-notch shows (some free), the shimmering interior with harbour vistas is worth stopping in for, or take a highly rec-

ommended 30-minute guided tour (1500kr); these run two to three times daily year-round, with up to eight daily tours between mid-June and mid-August.

Culture House   GALLERY

(Map p78; Þjóðmenningarhúsið; ☑530 2210; www.culturehouse.is; Hverfisgata 15; adult/child incl National Museum 2000kr/free; ⊙10am-5pm daily May–mid-Sep, closed Mon mid-Sep–Apr; ⊛) This fantastic collaboration between the National Museum, National Gallery and four other organisations creates a superbly curated exhibition covering the artistic and cultural heritage of Iceland from settlement to today. Priceless artefacts are arranged by theme, and highlights include 14th-century manuscripts, contemporary art, and the skeleton of a great auk (now extinct). Check the website for free guided tours.

Icelandic Phallological Museum   MUSEUM

(Map p74; Hið Íslenzka Reðasafn; ☑561 6663; www.phallus.is; Laugavegur 116; adult/child 1500kr/free; ⊙10am-6pm, from 9am Jun-Aug) Oh, the jokes are endless here, but although this unique museum houses a huge collection of penises, it's actually very well done. From pickled pickles to petrified wood, there are 286 different members on display, representing all Icelandic mammals and beyond. Featured items include contributions from sperm whales and a polar bear, minuscule mouse bits, silver castings of each member of the Icelandic handball team and a single human sample – from deceased mountaineer Páll Arason.

⊙ Laugardalur

★Laugardalur   AREA, PARK

(Map p74; ☑2, 5, 14, 15, 17) Laugardalur encompasses a verdant stretch of land 4km east of the city centre. It was once the main source of Reykjavík's hot-water supply: it translates as 'Hot-Springs Valley', and in the park's centre you'll find relics from the old wash house. The park is a favourite with locals for its huge swimming complex, fed by the geothermal spring, alongside a spa, cafe, skating rink, botanical gardens, sporting and concert arenas, and a zoo/entertainment park for kids.

Sigurjón Ólafsson Museum   GALLERY

(Map p74; Listasafn Sigurjóns Ólafssonar; ☑553 2906; www.lso.is; Laugarnestanga 70; adult/child 1000kr/free; ⊙1-5pm daily mid-May–mid-Sep, 2-5pm Sat & Sun mid-Sep–Nov & Feb–mid-May; ☑12, 16) Sculptor Sigurjón Ólafsson (1908–

82) used this peaceful seafront building as a studio. Now it showcases his varied, powerful work: portrait busts, driftwood totem poles and abstract pillars. A salty ocean breeze blows through the modern rooms, and the area is interlaced with waterfront paths giving clear views back to Reykjavík. Classical concerts (2500kr) are held in June and July on Tuesday at 8.30pm. The museum is a branch of the National Gallery; a combined ticket (1800kr) covers both museums plus the Ásgrímur Jónsson Collection.

🏃 Activities

Locally you can tour the city, rent bikes to zoom along lake or seaside trails, or pop into hot-pots all over town. Reykjavík is also the main hub for every kind of activity tour to all manner of destinations beyond the city limits. Most operators provide pick-up either from your accommodation or, if in the central zone, from a designated bus stop very nearby.

⭐ **Laugardalslaug**   GEOTHERMAL POOL, HOT-POT
(Map p74; ☑411 5100; www.reykjavik.is/stadir/laugardalslaug; Sundlaugavegur 30a, Laugardalur; adult/child 950/150kr, suit/towel rental 850/570kr; ⊙6.30am-10pm Mon-Fri, 8am-10pm Sat & Sun; ♿; 🚌12, 14) One of the largest pools in Iceland, with the best facilities: an Olympic-sized indoor pool and several outdoor pools, a string of hot-pots, a saltwater tub, a steam bath and a curling 86m water slide.

⭐ **Laugar Spa**   SPA, GYM
(Map p74; ☑553 0000; www.laugarspa.com; Sundlaugavegur 30a, Laugardalur; day pass 5800kr; ⊙6am-11pm Mon-Fri, 8am-9.30pm Sat & Sun) Super-duper Laugar Spa, next door to the Laugardalslaug geothermal pool, offers myriad ways to pamper yourself. There are six themed saunas and steam rooms, a seawater tub, a vast and well-equipped gym, fitness classes, and beauty and massage clinics with detox wraps, facials and hot-stone therapies. The spa is only open to visitors over 18; entry includes access to Laugardalslaug.

There's a cafe (dishes 2500 to 3000kr) and Icelandic-language child care.

Sundhöllin   GEOTHERMAL POOL
(Map p74; Sundhöll Reykjavíkur; ☑411 5350; www.reykjavik.is/stadir/sundholl-reykjavikur; Barónsstígur 16; adult/child 950/150kr; ⊙6.30am-10pm Mon-Fri, from 8am Sat & Sun; ♿) Our top pick for a Reykjavík city-centre swim. Sundhöll reopened in 2017 after a year-long revamp which added an entire outdoor area with hot tubs, sauna and a swimming pool. The original indoor

pool remains open, as does the secret upstairs hot tub with excellent city views.

Nauthólsvík Geothermal Beach   BEACH
(Map p74; ☑551 3177; www.nautholsvik.is; summer/winter free/600kr; ⊙10am-7pm mid-May–mid-Aug, 11am-1pm Mon-Fri, plus 5-7.30pm Mon & Wed, 11am-3pm Sat mid-Aug–mid-May; ♿; 🚌5) The small sandy arc of Nauthólsvík Geothermal Beach, on the edge of the Atlantic, gets packed on sunny summer days. During opening hours in summer only, geothermal water is routed in to keep the lagoon between 15°C and 19°C. There is also a busy hot-pot (38°C year-round), a snack bar and changing rooms.

👉 Tours

The tourist office (p86) has info on guided walking tours, plus loads of free maps and self-guided walking-tour brochures, from *Literary Reykjavík* to *The Neighbourhood of the Gods*. Hard-core walkers can buy the more in-depth *Reykjavík Walks* (2014; 3100kr) by Guðjón Friðriksson at local bookshops. There are downloadable smartphone apps, including Guides by Lonely Planet and Locatify (Smartguide).

⭐ **Literary Reykjavík**   WALKING
(Map p78; www.bokmenntaborgin.is; Tryggvagata 15; ⊙3pm Thu Jun-Aug) FREE The Dark Deeds city-centre walking tour focuses on crime fiction and starts at the main library. There's also a downloadable Culture Walks app and themes include Settlement, Crime Fiction and Queer Literature.

ℹ THE LOW-DOWN ON REYKJAVÍK'S POOLS

Reykjavík's naturally hot water is the heart of the city's social life (as in many Icelandic towns); children play, teenagers flirt, business deals are made and everyone catches up on the latest gossip at the baths. Volcanic heat keeps the temperature at a mellow 29°C, and most baths have *heitir pottar* (hot-pots): Jacuzzi-like pools kept a toasty 37°C to 42°C. Bring towels and bathing suits or rent them on-site. For further information and more locations, see www.spacity.is.

Reykjavikers get very upset by dirty tourists in their clean, chemical-free pools. To avoid causing huge offence, you must wash thoroughly with soap and without a swimsuit (yes, that means getting naked) before hopping in.

Reykjavík

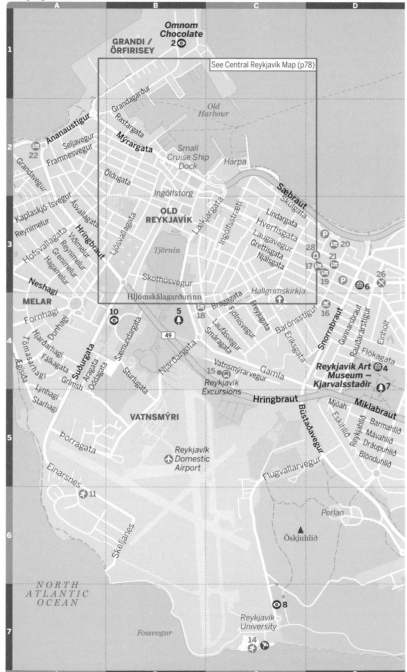

Omnom
Chocolate
2

GRANDI /
ÖRFIRISEY

See Central Reykjavík Map (p78)

Grandagarður

Old
Harbour

Rastargata

Ananaustigur

Seljavegur

Framnesvegur

Mýrargata

Small
Cruise Ship
Dock

Harpa

22

Grandavegur

Öldugata

Ingólfstorg

Sæbraut

Kaplaskjó-Isvegur

Ásvallagata

Hringbraut

Ljósvallagata

OLD
REYKJAVÍK

Lækjargata

Skúlagata

Lindargata

Hverfisgata

Laugavegur

Grettisgata

Njálsgata

28

20

Reynimelur

Hofsvallagata

Víðimelur

Reynimelur

Grenimelur

Hagamelur

Tjörnin

Ingólfsstræti

17

21

19

6

26

Neshagi

MELAR

Fornhagi

Skothúsvegur

Hljómskálagarðurinn

Bragagata

Hallgrímskirkja

Freyjugata

Barónsstígur

16

Dunhagi

10

5

18

Fjölnisvegur

Eiríksgata

Snorrabraut

Gunnarsbraut

Rauðarárstígur

Einholt

Hjarðarhagi

Tómasarhagi

Fálkagata

Grímsh

Aragata

Oldagata

Sæmundargata

49

Njarðargata

Laufásvegur

Smáragata

Flókagata

Ægisíða

Lynhagi

Starhagi

Suðurgata

Sturlugata

Vatnsmýrarvegur

Gamla

15

Reykjavík
Excursions

Reykjavík Art
Museum –
Kjarvalsstaðir

4

7

Hringbraut

Mjóah

Miklabraut

Barmahlíð

Bústaðavegur

Eskihlíð

Reykjahlíð

Mávahlíð

Dráupuhlíð

Blönduhlíð

VATNSMÝRI

Þorragata

Einarsnes

Reykjavík
Domestic
Airport

Flugvallarvegur

Perlan

11

Öskjuhlíð

Skeljanes

NORTH
ATLANTIC
OCEAN

8

Reykjavík
University

Fossvogur

14

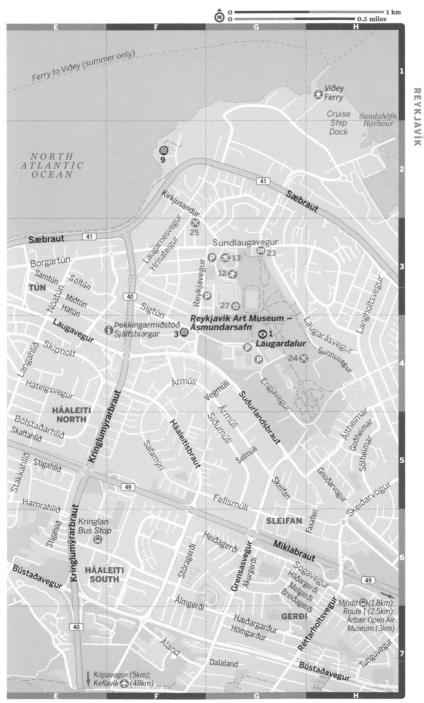

Reykjavík

★**Elding Adventures at Sea**   WILDLIFE
(Map p78; ☏519 5000; www.whalewatching.is; Ægisgarður 5; adult/child 11,000/5500kr; ☺harbour kiosk 8am-9pm; 🚌14) ✦ The city's most established and ecofriendly whale-watching tours feature a whale exhibition set in a converted fishing vessel; refreshments are sold on board. Elding also offers angling (adult/child 14,900/7450kr) and puffin-watching trips (adult/child from 6500/3250kr) and combo tours. It also runs the ferry to Viðey (☏533 5055; www.videy.com; Skarfabakki; return adult/child 1500/750kr; ☺from Skarfabakki hourly 10.15am-5.15pm mid-May–Sep, 1.15-4.30pm Sat & Sun Oct–mid-May). Pick-up available.

Free Walking Tour Reykjavik   WALKING
(Map p78; www.freewalkingtour.is; ☺noon & 2pm Jun-Aug, 1pm Sep-May) **FREE** A 90-minute, 1.5km walking tour of the city centre, starting at the little clock tower on Lækjartorg Sq.

Reykjavík Bike Tours   CYCLING
(Map p78; ☏694 8956; www.icelandbike.com; Ægisgarður 7; bike rental per 4hr from 3500kr, tours from 7500kr; ☺9am-5pm Jun-Aug, shorter hours Sep-May; 🚌14) This outfitter rents bikes and offers tours such as the Classic Reykjavík (2½ hours, 7km); Coast of Reykjavík (2½ hours, 18km); and Golden Circle & Bike (eight hours, 25km of cycling in 1½ hours). This is the most convenient place to rent a bike before catching the ferry to Viðey island.

🛏 Sleeping

June through August accommodation books out entirely; reservations are essential. Prices are high. Plan for hostels, camping or short-term apartment rentals to save money. Most places open year-round and many offer discounts or variable pricing online.

★**Reykjavík
Downtown Hostel**   HOSTEL **$**
(Map p78; ☏553 8120; www.hostel.is; Vesturgata 17; 4-/10-bed dm 9200/5700kr, d with/without bathroom 20,800/18,400kr; @🛜; 🚌14) The reviews are so good for this squeaky clean, charming and well-run hostel that it regularly lures large groups and the nonbackpacker set. Enjoy friendly service, a guest kitchen and excellent rooms. Discount 800kr for HI members.

★**KEX Hostel**   HOSTEL **$**
(Map p74; ☏561 6060; www.kexhostel.is; Skúlagata 28; 4-/16-bed dm 7900/4800kr, d with/without bathroom 34,500/20,000kr; @🛜) An unofficial headquarters of backpackerdom and popular local gathering place, KEX is a megahostel with heaps of sociability and style (think retro vaudeville meets rodeo). The bathrooms may be shared by many, but KEX remains a favourite for its lively restaurant-bar with interior courtyard and water views.

Oddsson Hostel   HOSTEL **$**
(Map p74; ☏511 3579; www.oddsson.is; Hringbraut 121; dm from 6000kr, d with/without bathroom

32,340/24,500kr; 🛜; 💻14) You can't miss this large, quirky hostel near the Old Harbour with its brightly coloured facade. There are dorm rooms, tiny private pod-like doubles and regular hotel rooms, some with excellent sea views. Everyone shares a kitchen, hot tub, rooftop, and yoga and karaoke rooms.

★ Nest Apartments   APARTMENT $$
(Map p78; 📞893 0280; www.nestapartments.is; Bergthorugata 15; apt from 20,000kr; 🛜) Four thoroughly modern apartments with neat antique touches make a superb home away from home on this central, peaceful street. Ranged over a tall townhouse, the apartments sleep two to four people – the one in the loft steals the show with water and mountain views. There's a two-night minimum.

★ Loft Hostel   HOSTEL $$
(Map p78; 📞553 8140; www.lofthostel.is; Bankastræti 7; dm 8500-9900kr; d/q 26,200/36,700kr; @🛜) Perched high above the action on bustling Bankastræti, this modern hostel attracts a decidedly young crowd, including locals who come for its trendy bar and cafe terrace. This sociable spot comes with neat dorms with linen included and en suite bathrooms.

Forsæla Apartmenthouse   GUESTHOUSE, APARTMENT $$
(Map p78; 📞551 6046; www.apartmenthouse.is; Grettisgata 33b; d/tr without bathroom incl breakfast 25,700/34,500kr, apt/house from 45,150/90,300kr; 🛜📶) A 100-year-old wood-and-tin house is the star of the show here. It sleeps four to eight people and comes with old beams and tasteful mod cons. Smaller apartments have cosy bedrooms and sitting rooms, kitchens and washing machines. Or opt for the B&B lodging alongside. There's a minimum three-night stay.

Grettir Apartments   APARTMENT $$
(Map p74; 📞694 7020; contact@grettisborg.is; Grettisgata 53b; apt 23,500-57,700kr; 🛜📶) Sleeping here is like sleeping in a magazine for Scandinavian home design. The thoroughly modern studios and apartments boast fine furnishings and sleek built-ins. The largest sleeps six or seven.

REY Apartments   APARTMENT $$
(Map p78; 📞771 4600; www.rey.is; Grettisgata 2a; apt 30,000-55,800kr; 🛜📶) For those preferring private digs over hotel stays, REY is a smart choice thanks to its cache of modern,

two- to eight-person apartments scattered across several Escher-like stairwells. They're well maintained and stylishly decorated.

Luna Hotel Apartments   APARTMENT $$
(Map p74; 📞852 7572; www.luna.is; reception 3rd fl, Laugavegur 77; apt from 24,200kr) A strong entry on Reykjavík's luxury-apartment scene, Luna maintains 15 excellent apartments in the streets near Skólavörðustígur. Locations are relatively quiet, and the apartments are bright and cheerful, ranging from small studios to four-bedroom pads that sleep eight.

Hótel Reykjavík Centrum   HOTEL $$
(Map p78; 📞514 6000; www.hotelcentrum.is; Aðalstræti 16; d/apt/ste from 27,400/39,300/51,800kr; 📶🛜) Mezzanines and a glass roof unite two historic buildings, giving this hotel a spry, light feel. Its 89 neatly proportioned rooms, suites and apartments all have mini-fridges, satellite TV and coffee-making gear. Prices vary wildly online depending on date.

Baldursbrá Guesthouse   GUESTHOUSE $$
(Map p78; 📞552 6646; baldursbra@centrum.is; Laufásvegur 41; s/d/tr without bathroom incl breakfast from 9,700/17,800/19,000kr; 🛜) Decent-sized comfy rooms with washbasins characterise this little guesthouse on a quiet street near Tjörnin. You'll also find a sitting room and garden with hot-pot and barbecue. The owners provide friendly, attentive service.

Castle House Apartments   APARTMENT $$
(Map p78; 📞511 2166; www.hotelsiceland.net; Skálholtsstígur 2a; apt from 20,500kr; 🛜📶) Modern, self-contained apartments are satisfyingly central and commendably quiet. More personal than a hotel, they still come with room service: fresh towels appear daily and washing up seems to magically look after itself. The same people run **Embassy Apartments** (Map p78; 📞511 2166; Garðastræti 40; apt from 24,400kr; 🛜) on the northwest side of Tjörnin.

ⓘ SHORT-TERM RENTALS

Reykjavík's sky-high summertime accommodation prices have led enterprising locals in the capital's prized neighbourhoods to rent their apartments (or rooms) to short-stay visitors. Prices often beat commercial rates, though of course there's no maid, concierge etc. Aim for a Reykjavík 101 postal code to be centrally located.

Central Reykjavík

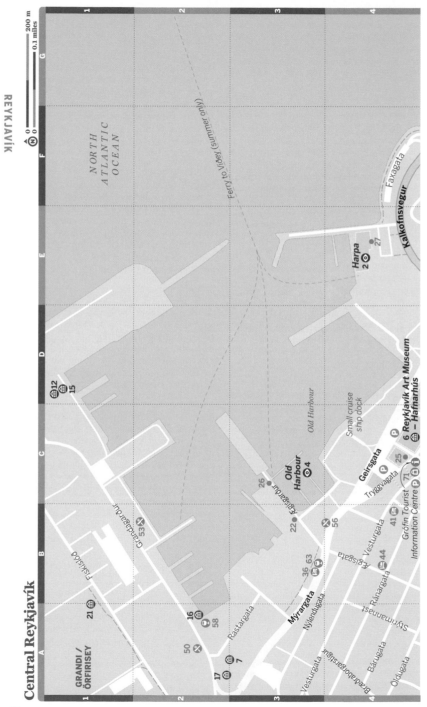

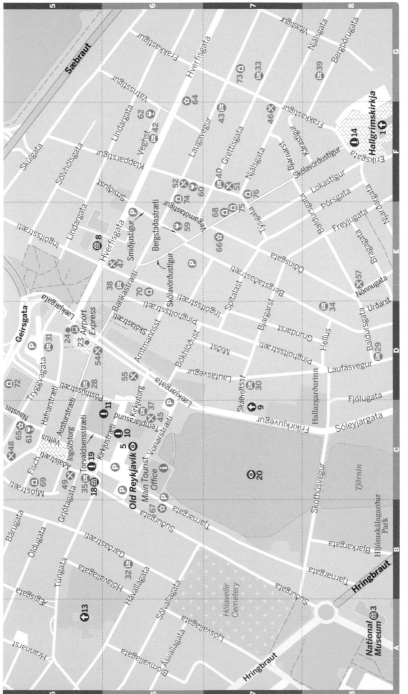

79

Central Reykjavík

Galtafell Guesthouse GUESTHOUSE $$
(Map p74; ☑699 2525; www.galtafell.com; Laufásvegur 46; d with/without bathroom from 25,300/24,600kr, apt from 29,000kr; ☞) The four one-bedroom apartments in this converted historic mansion have fully equipped kitchens, cosy seating areas and the use of a lovely garden. The three double rooms share a guest kitchen. It's all tucked away in a quiet lakeside neighbourhood within easy walking distance of the city centre.

Reykjavík City Hostel HOSTEL $$
(Map p74; ☑553 8110; www.hostel.is; Sundlaugavegur 34; dm from 4500kr, d with/without bathroom 23,100/19,100kr; ⓟ@☞❖; ☐14) ⚑ Reykjavík's original hostel is a large, ecofriendly complex with a fun backpacker vibe. Two kilometres east of the city centre in Laugardalur, it abuts the swimming pool, and is served by the Flybus and many tour operators. It boasts bike rental, guest kitchen, barbecue and spacious deck.

Three Sisters APARTMENT $$
(Map p78; Þrjár Systur; ☑565 2181; www.threesisters.is; Ránargata 16; 2-/4-person apt 24,400/49,800kr; ☺mid-May–Aug; @☞❖) A welcoming owner who goes the extra mile to meet guests' needs lifts Three Sisters above the crowd. The seven studio apartments in the corner townhouse have comfy beds, homey decor, flat-screen TVs and kitchens.

★Alda Hotel BOUTIQUE HOTEL $$$
(Map p74; ☑553 9366; www.aldahotel.is; Laugavegur 66; d/tr 40,500/47,400kr, ste from 87,300kr; ☞) A wealth of boutique touches lift sleek Alda well above the crowd: knitted lamp covers, a sauna and hot tub, and the free cell phones given to guests (all local calls and data are free). The vast King suite is made sumptuous by a huge TV, coffee machine and free-standing slipper bath.

★Consulate
Hotel Reykjavík LUXURY HOTEL $$$
(Map p78; ☑514 6800; www.curiocollection3. hilton.com; Hafnarstraeti 17; d incl breakfast from 44,700kr, ste from 112,700kr; ❋@☞) Hilton's new Curio hotel is a plush place where the service is impeccable and conversations are held in quiet tones. A supremely sympathetic conversion of a 1900s department store has created welcoming bedrooms rich in antique flourishes and modern comforts – espresso machines, blackout curtains and big TVs. There's also a gym and spa.

Apotek   BOUTIQUE HOTEL **$$$**

(Map p78; ☑512 9000; www.keahotels.is; Austurstræti 16; d incl breakfast from 42,200kr; 🛜) Set in one of the city's most iconic buildings – a well-renovated former pharmacy smack in the centre of Old Reykjavík, which dates from 1917 and was designed by Guðjón Samúelsson. It offers slick contemporary rooms in muted tones and a popular ground-floor tapas-style restaurant-bar (p83).

Kvosin Downtown   HOTEL **$$$**

(Map p78; ☑571 4460; www.kvosinhotel.is; Kirkjutorg 4; 2-/4-/6-person ste incl breakfast 43,600/49,800/67,300kr; 🛜) Firmly a part of Reykjavík's luxury-accommodation wave, the suites at this superbly located historic hotel range from 'Junior' and 'Executive' to 'Valkyrie'. Espresso machines adorn the kitchenettes and all the mod cons are standard, including Sóley toiletries.

Icelandair Hotel

Reykjavík Marina   BOUTIQUE HOTEL **$$$**

(Map p78; ☑booking 444 000, hotel 560 8000; www.icelandairhotels.is; Mýrargata 2; d 34,850-42,500kr, ste from 47,600kr; @🛜; 🚌14) Captivating art, cool nautical-chic decor and up-to-the-second mod cons ensure this harbourside design hotel is a gorgeous retreat. Clever ways to conserve space make the small rooms winners. The attic bedrooms facing the harbour have excellent sea views. The lobby is home to the happening Slippbarinn cocktail bar (p84).

Reykjavík Residence   APARTMENT **$$$**

(Map p78; ☑561 1200; www.rrhotel.is; Hverfisgata 45; 2-/3-/8-person apt 33,500/37,300/87,000kr; @🛜♿) Plush city-centre living feels just right in this array of apartments set in six historic mansions. Linens are crisp, service attentive and the light a glowing gold. The pick of the lot are the Royal Suites in the former home of an Icelandic prime minister – named after one-time visitors, the king and queen of Denmark

Hótel Holt   LUXURY HOTEL **$$$**

(Map p78; ☑552 5700; www.holt.is; Bergstaðastræti 37; s 31,000-34,000kr, d 35,000-45,000kr; @🛜) Expect a totally cool blast from the luxurious past. Built in the 1960s as one of Reykjavík's first hotels, Holt is decked out with original paintings, drawings and sculptures (it boasts the largest private art collection in Iceland), set off by warm-toned decor.

Sandhotel BOUTIQUE HOTEL $$$
(Map p78; ☏519 8090; www.sandhotel.is; Laugavegur 34; r from 40,000kr; ☏) When the folks behind one of Iceland's best bakeries (p88) open a hotel, you know it's going to be great. At Sandhotel art deco echoes meet Nordic design and 21st-century luxury: in-room espresso machines, bluetooth speakers, fine linens and soft towels. The breakfast breads and pastries are, of course, superb.

✕ Eating

From hot dogs to gourmet platters on white-clothed tables, little Reykjavík has an astonishing assortment of eateries. Loads of seafood and Icelandic or 'New Nordic' restaurants serve tried-and-true variations on local fish and lamb, but the capital is also the main spot for finding international eats.

Kolaportið Flea Market (p86) also has a section with traditional Icelandic foods.

★ Grandi Mathöll STREET FOOD $
(Map p78; ☏577 6200; www.grandimatholl.is; Grandagarður 16; mains from 1200kr; ⊙11am-9pm Mon-Thu, to 10pm Fri-Sun) There's no neater encapsulation of Grandi's rejuvenation than the transformation of this old fish factory into a pioneering street-food hall. Long trestle tables sit beside stalls selling a diverse range of lamb, fish and veggie delights; look out for the Gastro Truck, its succulent signature chicken burger has quite a jalapeño kick.

★ Sægreifinn SEAFOOD $
(Map p78; Seabaron; ☏553 1500; www.saegreifinn.is; Geirsgata 8; mains from 1500kr; ⊙11.30am-10pm) Sidle into this green harbourside shack for the most famous lobster soup in the capital, or choose from a fridge full of fresh fish skewers to be grilled on the spot. Though the original sea baron sold the restaurant some years ago, the place retains its unfussy, down-to-earth charm.

★ Flatey Pizza PIZZA $
(Map p78; ☏588 2666; www.flatey.pizza; Grandagarður 11; pizzas 1750-2650kr; ⊙11am-10pm) Flatey raises pizza making to something akin to an art form. Its sourdough circles are made from organic wheat and are baked for just one minute at 500°C to keep the toppings tasty. It's very hip and very classy. As you can't book, be prepared to queue.

Gló ORGANIC, VEGETARIAN $
(Map p78; ☏553 1111; www.glo.is; Laugavegur 20b; mains 1000-2400kr; ⊙11.30am-10pm; ☏✎) Join the cool cats in this airy upstairs restaurant serving fresh daily specials loaded with Asian-influenced herbs and spices. Though not exclusively vegetarian, it's a wonderland of raw and organic foods, with a broad bar of elaborate salads, from root veggies to Greek.

Bakarí Sandholt BAKERY $
(Map p78; ☏551 3524; www.sandholt.is; Laugavegur 36; snacks 700-2700kr; ⊙7am-7pm Sun-Thu, 6.30am-9pm Fri & Sat; ☏) Reykjavík's favourite bakery is usually crammed with folks hoovering up the generous assortment of fresh baguettes, croissants, pastries and sandwiches. The soup of the day (1850kr) comes with delicious sourdough bread.

Brauð & Co BAKERY $
(Map p78; www.braudogco.is; Frakkastígur 16; ⊙6am-6pm Mon-Fri, to 5pm Sat & Sun) Head for the building smothered in rainbow paint then queue for the locals' tip for the best snúður (cinnamon buns) in town – watch Viking hipsters make them while you wait.

Frú Lauga MARKET $
(Map p74; ☏534 7165; www.frulauga.is; Laugalækur 6; ⊙10am-6pm Mon-Fri, to 4pm Sat; ✎) ✎ Reykjavík's trailblazing farmers market sources its ingredients from all over the countryside, featuring treats such as skyr (Icelandic yoghurt) from Erpsstaðir, organic vegetables, rhubarb conserves, honey and meat. It also stocks a range of carefully curated international pastas, chocolates and wine.

Garðurinn VEGETARIAN $
(Map p78; ☏561 2345; www.kaffigardurinn.is; Klapparstígur 37; mains 1400-2200kr; ⊙11am-8.30pm Mon, Tue, Thu & Fri, to 5pm Wed, noon-5pm Sat; ✎) Asian, Middle Eastern and Mediterranean flavours infuse ever-changing vegetarian and vegan soups (950kr) and dishes of the day at this friendly eatery.

★ Messinn SEAFOOD $$
(Map p78; ☏546 0095; www.messinn.com; Lækjargata 6b; lunch mains 1850-2200kr, dinner mains 2700-4200kr; ⊙11.30am-3pm & 5-10pm; ☏) Make a beeline to Messinn for the best seafood that Reykjavík has to offer. The speciality here is the amazing pan-fried dishes: your pick of fish is served up in a sizzling cast-iron skillet, accompanied

by buttery potatoes and salad. The mood is upbeat and comfortable and the staff friendly.

★ Matur og Drykkur   ICELANDIC $$

(Map p78; [☎]571 8877; www.maturogdrykkur. is; Grandagarður 2; lunch/dinner mains from 1900/3400kr, tasting menu 10,000kr; [⏰]11.30am-3pm & 6-10pm, closed Sun lunch; [🅿]; [🚌]14) One of Reykjavík's top high-concept restaurants, Matur Og Drykkur means 'Food and Drink', and you'll surely be plied with the best of both. The brainchild of brilliant chef Gísli Matthías Auðunsson, who also owns the excellent Slippurinn (p28), it creates inventive versions of traditional Icelandic fare. Book ahead in high season and for dinner.

Hlemmur Mathöll   FOOD HALL $$

(Map p74; www.hlemmurmatholl.is; Laugavegur 107; mains from 800kr; [⏰]8am-11pm) If only all bus terminals had a food court like this. Some 10 vendors rustle up multicultural foods including Danish *smørrebrød* (rye bread), Mexican tacos and Vietnamese street food. The pick is innovative SKÁL!. Most stalls kick into action by lunchtime.

SKÁL!   STREET FOOD $$

(Map p74; [☎]775 2299; www.skalrvk.com; Laugavegur 107; mains 1000-2500kr; [⏰]noon-10pm Sun-Wed, to 11pm Thu-Sat; [🅿]) SKÁL! demands your attention – with its capital lettering and punctuation but most emphatically with its food. Experimental offerings combine unusual flavours (fermented garlic, birch sugar, arctic thyme salt) with Icelandic ingredients to impressive effect, best sampled at a stool beside its neon-topped bar. There's an impressive list of vegan creations and the cocktails feature foraged herbs.

Café Flóra   CAFE $$

(Map p74; Flóran; [☎]553 8872; www.floran.is; Botanic Gardens; cakes from 950kr, mains 1550-3150kr; [⏰]8am-10pm May-Sep; [🅿]) 🥬 Sun-dappled tables fill a greenhouse in the Botanic Gardens and spill onto a flower-lined terrace at this lovely cafe specialising in wholesome local ingredients – some grown in the gardens themselves. Soups come with sourdough bread, while snacks range from cheese platters with nuts and honey to pulled-pork sandwiches. Weekend brunch, good coffee and homemade cakes round it all out.

★ Dill   ICELANDIC $$$

(Map p78; [☎]552 1522; www.dillrestaurant.is; Hverfisgata 12; 5/7 courses 11,900/13,900kr; [⏰]6-10pm Wed-Sat) Exquisite 'New Nordic' cuisine is the major drawcard at Reykjavík's elegant Michelin-starred bistro. Skilled chefs use a small number of ingredients to create highly complex dishes in a parade of courses. The owners are friends with Copenhagen's famous Noma clan and take Icelandic cuisine to similarly heady heights. It's hugely popular; book well in advance.

★ Apotek   FUSION $$$

([☎]551 0011; www.apotekrestaurant.is; Austurstræti 16; mains 2800-6000kr; [⏰]noon-11pm Sun-Thu, to midnight Fri & Sat) This beautiful restaurant and bar with shining glass fixtures and a cool ambience is equally known for its delicious menu of small plates that are perfect for sharing and its top-flight cocktails. It's on the ground floor of the hotel of the same name.

★ Grillmarkaðurinn   FUSION $$$

(Map p78; Grill Market; [☎]571 7777; www.grillmarkadurinn.is; Lækjargata 2a; mains 3500-9500kr; [⏰]11.30am-2pm Mon-Fri, 6-10.30pm daily) Topnotch dining is the order of the day here, from the moment you enter the glass atrium with its golden-globe lights to your first snazzy cocktail, and on throughout the meal. Service is impeccable, and locals and visitors alike rave about the food, which uses Icelandic ingredients prepared with culinary imagination by master chefs.

Fiskfélagið   SEAFOOD $$$

(Map p78; [☎]552 5300; www.fishcompany.is; Vesturgata 2a; mains lunch 2700-4600kr, dinner 4800-6600kr; [⏰]11.30am-2.30pm Mon-Fri, 5.30-10.30pm daily) The 'Fish Company' takes Icelandic seafood recipes and spins them through a variety of far-flung inspirations from Fiji coconut to Spanish chorizo. Dine out on the terrace or in an intimate-feeling stone-and-timber room with copper light fittings and quirky furnishings.

Fiskmarkaðurinn   SEAFOOD $$$

(Map p78; Fishmarket; [☎]578 8877; www.fiskmarkadurinn.is; Aðalstræti 12; mains 4800-9900kr, tasting menu 11,900kr; [⏰]5-10.30pm) Dramatic presentations of elaborate dishes fill the tables of this intimate, artistically lit restaurant, where chefs excel at infusing Icelandic seafood with Asian flavours such as lotus root. The tasting menu is acclaimed, and the place is renowned for its excellent sushi bar (3600kr to 4100kr).

Þrír Frakkar ICELANDIC, SEAFOOD $$$
(Map p78; ☑ 552 3939; www.facebook.com/
3frakkar.is; Baldursgata 14; mains 4200-6250kr;
⏱11.30am-2.30pm & 6-10pm Mon-Fri, 6-11pm Sat &
Sun) Owner-chef Úlfar Eysteinsson has built
up a consistently excellent reputation at
this snug little restaurant. Specialities range
throughout the aquatic world from salt cod
and halibut to *plokkfiskur* (fish stew) with
black bread. Non-fish items run towards
guillemot, horse, lamb and whale.

🍷 Drinking & Nightlife

Sometimes it's hard to distinguish between
cafes, restaurants and bars in Reykjavík, be-
cause when night rolls around (whether light
or dark out) many coffee shops and bistros
turn lights down and volume up, swapping
cappuccinos for cocktails. Craft-beer bars,
high-end cocktail bars and music and dance
venues flesh out the scene. Some hotels and
hostels also have trendy bars.

★**Kaldi** BAR
(Map p78; ☑ 581 2200; www.kaldibar.is; Laugavegur
20b; ⏱noon-1am Sun-Thu, to 3am Fri & Sat) Effort-
lessly cool with mismatched seats and teal
banquettes, plus a popular smoking court-
yard, Kaldi is awesome for its range of five
Kaldi microbrews, not available elsewhere.
Happy hour (4pm to 7pm) gets you a beer for
750kr. Anyone can play the in-house piano.

★**Mikkeller & Friends** CRAFT BEER
(Map p78; ☑ 437 0203; www.mikkeller.dk; Hverfis-
gata 12; ⏱5pm-1am Sun-Thu, 2pm-1am Fri & Sat;
☎) Climb to the top floor of this building

to find a Danish craft-beer pub with 20 taps
serving Mikkeller's own offerings and local
Icelandic brews. Then enjoy the cool, colour-
ful, laid-back vibe.

Bryggjan Brugghús CRAFT BEER
(Map p78; ☑ 456 4040; www.bryggjanbrugghus.is;
Grandagarður 8; ⏱11am-midnight Sun-Thu, to 1am
Fri & Sat; ☎) Cavernous, dimly lit and dotted
with vintage pub paraphernalia, harbourside
Bryggjan Brugghús is a roomy microbrewery
where 12 taps dispense its own fresh-tasting
beers. Join one of the regular **brewery tours**
(☑ 456 4040; tours 3500-5000kr; ⏱noon-10pm)
then settle back to sip a house beer – 600kr
during happy hour (3pm to 7pm).

Paloma CLUB
(Map p78; http://palomaclub.is; Naustin 1; ⏱8pm-
1am Thu & Sun, to 4.30am Fri & Sat) At one of Rey-
kjavík's best late-night dance clubs DJs lay
down reggae, electronica and pop upstairs,
and a dark deep house dance scene in the
basement.

Slippbarinn COCKTAIL BAR
(Map p78; ☑ 560 8080; www.slippbarinn.is; Mýrarga-
ta 2; ⏱noon-midnight Sun-Thu, to 1am Fri & Sat; ☎)
Jet-setters unite at this buzzy bar at the Old
Harbour's Icelandair Hotel Reykjavík Marina
(p81). It's bedecked with vintage record play-
ers and cool locals sipping some of the best
cocktails in town. For cut-price creations drop
by during happy hour (3pm to 6pm).

Kaffibarinn BAR
(Map p78; ☑ 551 1588; www.kaffibarinn.is; Berg-
staðastræti 1; ⏱3pm-1am Sun-Thu, to 4.30am Fri

DJAMMIÐ: HOW TO PARTY IN REYKJAVÍK

Reykjavík is renowned for its weekend party scene that goes strong into the wee hours,
and even spills over onto some of the weekdays (especially in summer). *Djammið* in the
capital means 'going out on the town', or you could say *pöbbarölt* for a 'pub stroll'.

Thanks to the high price of alcohol, things generally don't get going until late. Iceland-
ers brave the melee at the government alcohol store Vínbúðin (www.vinbudin.is), then
toddle home for a prepub party. People hit town around midnight, party until 5am, queue
for a hot dog, then topple into bed.

Rather than settling into one venue for the evening, Icelanders like to cruise from bar to
bar, getting progressively louder and less inhibited as the evening goes on. 'In' clubs may
have long queues, but they tend to move quickly with the constant circulation of revellers.

Most of the action is concentrated near Laugavegur and Austurstræti. Places usually
stay open until 1am Sunday to Thursday and 4am or 5am on Friday and Saturday. You'll
pay around 1200kr to 1600kr per pint of beer, and drinks hit the 2000kr to 2800kr
mark. Some venues have cover charges (around 1000kr) after midnight, and many have
early-in-the-evening happy hours that cut costs by 500kr or 700kr per beer. Download
the smartphone app Reykjavík Appy Hour.

The legal drinking age is 20 years.

& Sat; 🛜) This old house with the London Underground symbol over the door contains one of Reykjavík's coolest bars; it even had a starring role in the cult movie *101 Reykjavík* (2000). At weekends you'll feel like you need either a famous face or a battering ram to get in. At other times it's a place for artistic types to chill with their Macs.

Port 9   WINE BAR
(Map p78; 📞832 2929; www.facebook.com/port niu; Veghúsastígur 7; ⏱4-11pm Tue-Sat, to 9pm Sun & Mon) Port 9 sauntered onto Reykjavík's drinking scene supremely confident in the quality of its wines and the knowledge of its staff – offerings here range from affordable tipples by the glass to vintages to break the bank. Low lighting, an arty clientele and a secret hang-out vibe (it's tucked down a tiny street) make it worth tracking down.

☆ Entertainment

The ever-changing and vibrant Reykjavík performing-arts scene features shows at bars and cafes, local theatres and the Harpa concert hall. For the latest in Icelandic music and performing arts, and to see who's playing, consult free English-language newspaper *Grapevine* (www.grapevine.is) and its events listing app Appening; websites Visit Reykjavík (www.visitreykjavik.is), What's On in Reykjavík (www.whatson.is/magazine) and Musik.is (www.musik.is); or city music shops.

★Húrra   LIVE MUSIC
(Map p78; www.facebook.com/hurra.is; Tryggvagata 22; ⏱6pm-1am Mon-Thu, to 4.30am Fri & Sat, to 11.30pm Sun; 🛜) Dark and raw, this large bar opens up its back room to create a much-loved concert venue, with a wide range of live music or DJs most nights. It's one of the best places in town to close out the evening. There's a range of beers on tap and happy hour runs till 9pm.

★Bíó Paradís   CINEMA
(Map p78; 📞412 7711; www.bioparadis.is; Hverfisgata 54; adult 1600-1800kr; 🛜) This totally cool cinema, decked out in movie posters and vintage officeware, screens specially curated Icelandic films with English subtitles and international flicks. It's a chance to see movies that you may not find elsewhere.

Tjarnarbíó   THEATRE
(Map p78; 📞527 2100; www.tjarnarbio.is; Tjarnargata 12; tickets from 2000kr) Drama, stand-up comedy, improv and dance all get a showing at this long-standing, independent perform-

ing arts theatre. Look out for the many shows performed in English. The vibrant theatre cafe-bar is open during the day, too.

Mengi   LIVE PERFORMANCE
(Map p78; 📞588 3644; www.mengi.net; Óðinsgata 2; ⏱noon-5pm Tue-Sat & for performances) It's small, but Mengi offers an innovative program of music and visual and performing arts.

🛍 Shopping

Reykjavík's vibrant design culture makes for great shopping: from sleek fish-skin purses and knitted *lopapeysur* (Icelandic woollen sweaters) to unique music or Icelandic schnapps *brennivín*. Laugavegur is the most dense shopping street. You'll find interesting shops all over town, but fashion concentrates near the Frakkastígur and Vitastígur end of Laugavegur. Skólavörðustígur is strong for arts and jewellery, while Bankastræti and Austurstræti have touristy shops.

All visitors are eligible for a 15% tax refund on their shopping, under certain conditions.

★Fischer   CONCEPT STORE
(Map p78; www.fischersund.com; Fischersund 3; ⏱noon-6pm Mon-Sat) Formally the recording studio of Icelandic musician Jónsi, best known as the Sigur Rós frontman, this concept store feels like walking through an immersive exhibition. Perfumes, Icelandic herbs, hand-crafted soap bars and candles, ethereal music and visual artwork play with all the senses.

★Kirsuberjatréð   ARTS & CRAFTS
(Map p78; Cherry Tree; 📞562 8990; www.kirs.is; Vesturgata 4; ⏱10am-7pm Mon-Fri, to 5pm Sat & Sun) Talented designers show their works at this long-running women's art-and-design collective. Highlights include the bracelets and purses made from soft, supple, brightly coloured fish-skin leather, music boxes made from string, and, our favourite, beautiful coloured bowls made from radish slices.

★**Kolaportið Flea Market**　　　MARKET
(Map p78; www.kolaportid.is; Tryggvagata 19; ⊙11am-5pm Sat & Sun) Kolaportið is a Reykjavík institution. Weekends see a huge industrial building by the harbour filled with a vast tumble of secondhand clothes, old toys and cheap imports. A food section sells traditional eats like *rúgbrauð* (geothermally baked rye bread) and *brauðterta* ('sandwich cake'; a layering of bread with mayonnaise-based fillings).

Skúmaskot　　　ARTS & CRAFTS
(Map p78; ☑663 1013; www.facebook.com/sku maskot.art.design; Skólavörðustígur 21a; ⊙10am-6pm Mon-Fri, to 5pm Sat, noon-4pm Sun) Local designers create unique handmade porcelain items, women's and kids' clothing, paintings and cards. It's in a large renovated gallery that beautifully showcases the creative Icelandic crafts.

KronKron　　　CLOTHING
(Map p74; ☑561 9388; www.kronkron.com; Laugavegur 63b; ⊙10am-6pm Mon-Fri, to 5pm Sat) This is where Reykjavík goes high fashion, with labels such as Marc Jacobs and Vivienne Westwood. But we really enjoy its Scandinavian designers (including Kron by KronKron) and the offering of silk dresses, knit capes, scarves and even woollen underwear. The handmade shoes are off the charts; they are also sold down the street at **Kron** (Map p78; ☑551 8388; www.kron.is; Laugavegur 48; ⊙10am-6pm Mon-Fri, to 5pm Sat).

Kiosk　　　CLOTHING
(Map p78; ☑571 3636.; www.kioskreykjavik.com; Ingólfsstræti 6; ⊙11am-6pm Mon-Fri, to 5pm Sat) This wonderful designers' cooperative is lined with creative women's fashion in a glass-fronted boutique. Designers take turns staffing the store.

Orrifinn　　　JEWELLERY
(Map p78; ☑789 7616; www.orrifinn.com; Skólavörðustígur 17a; ⊙10am-6pm Mon-Fri, 11am-4pm Sat) Orrifinn's subtle, beautiful jewellery captures the natural wonder of Iceland and its Viking history. Delicate anchors, axes and pen nibs dangle from understated matte chains. There are some workbenches here so you're likely to see the jewellers creating pieces.

12 Tónar　　　MUSIC
(Map p78; ☑511 5656; www.12tonar.is; Skólavörðustígur 15; ⊙10am-6pm Mon-Sat, from noon Sun) A very cool place to hang out; in two-storey 12 Tónar you can listen to CDs, drink coffee and on summer Fridays sometimes you can catch a live performance. It is

responsible for launching some of Iceland's favourite bands.

Mál og Menning　　　BOOKS
(Map p78; ☑580 5000; www.bmm.is; Laugavegur 18; ⊙9am-10pm Mon-Fri, 10am-10pm Sat; ☎) A friendly, well-stocked independent bookshop that has a strong selection of Englishlanguage books offering insights into Iceland. It also sells maps, CDs, games and newspapers and has a good cafe (soup and bread 1000kr).

❶ Information

Grófin Tourist Information Centre (Map p78; Iceland Travel Assistance Head Office; ☑570 7700; www.ita.is; Grófin 1; ⊙8am-8pm) Large tourist information centre with friendly staff, currency exchange, printing and luggage storage. Under the wing of Iceland Travel Assistance, running several outlets in Reykjavík, it acts primarily as a booking service. For specific travel advice, head for the publicly funded Main Tourist Office.

Landspítali University Hospital (☑543 1000, doctor on duty 1770; www.landspitali.is; Fossvogur) Casualty department open 24/7.

Main Tourist Office (Map p78; Upplýsingamiðstöð Ferðamanna; ☑411 6040; www.visitreykjavik.is; Ráðhús, Tjarnargata 11; ⊙8am-8pm; ☎) The city's official tourist office is located in the Ráðhús (City Hall). Friendly staff and mountains of free brochures, plus maps, the Reykjavík City Card and Strætó city bus tickets for sale. Books accommodation, tours and activities too. The SafeTravel desk, an initiative led by the Icelandic Search & Rescue, is gold for those planning outdoor adventures such as overnight hikes or driving in the highlands.

Police Station (☑emergency 112, nonemergency 444 1000; Hverfisgata 113) Central police station.

Reykjavík City Card (www.citycard.is; 24/48/72hr 3800/5400/6500kr) Offers admission to Reykjavík's 18 municipal swimming and thermal pools and to most of the main galleries and museums, plus discounts on some tours, shops and entertainment. Also gives free travel on the city's Strætó buses and on the ferry to Viðey. Available at the Main Tourist Office, some travel agencies, 10-11 supermarkets, HI hostels and some hotels.

❶ Getting There & Around

AIR
Iceland's primary international airport, Keflavík International Airport (p112), is 48km west of Reykjavík, on the Reykjanes Peninsula.

TRANSPORT TO/FROM KEFLAVÍK INTERNATIONAL AIRPORT

The journey from Keflavík International Airport to Reykjavík takes about 50 minutes. Three easy bus services connect Reykjavík and the airport and are the best transport option; kids get discounted fares.

Flybus (⌨ 580 5400; www.re.is; one-way ticket 2950kr; 📶) Meets all international flights. Hotel pick-up/drop off costs 3950kr and shuttles you from/to the Flybus at the BSÍ bus terminal; book hotel pick-up at least a day ahead. A separate service runs to the Blue Lagoon (4990kr), from where you can continue to the city centre or the airport. Buy tickets online, at many hotels, or at the airport booth. Flybus will also drop off/pick up in Garðabær and Hafnarfjörður, just south of Reykjavík. It's operated by Reykjavík Excursions (p27).

Airport Express (⌨ 540 1313; www.airportexpress.is; 📶) Links the airport with Lækjartorg Sq (2700kr) in central Reykjavík or Mjódd bus terminal, or via hotel pick-up/drop off (3300kr; book ahead). Also has connections to Borgarnes and points north, including Akureyri. Operated by **Grayline Iceland** (Iceland Excursions; ⌨ 540 1313; www.grayline.is; Hafnarstræti 20).

Airport Direct (⌨ 497 5000; www.reykjaviksightseeing.is/airport-direct; one way/return from 5500/10,000kr; 📶) Minibuses operated by Reykjavík Sightseeing link accommodation and the airport.

Strætó bus 55 also connects the BSÍ bus terminal and the airport (1840kr, 1¼ hours, nine daily Monday to Friday). Taxis from Keflavík airport to Reykjavík cost around 16,100kr.

Reykjavík Domestic Airport (p112) is in central Reykjavík, just 2km south of Tjörnin. Sightseeing services, domestic flights and those to/from Greenland and the Faroe Islands fly here. From this airport it's a 2km walk into town. Otherwise bus 15 goes to the Hlemmur bus stop. A cab into the city centre costs around 1300kr.

BICYCLE

Reykjavík has a steadily improving network of cycle lanes; ask the Main Tourist Office for a map. You are allowed to cycle on pavements as long as you don't cause pedestrians problems.

The bike-share scheme **WOW City Bike** (⌨ 590 3085; www.wowcitybike.com; per hr 850kr) has docks in eight places around town. Or you can rent from Reykjavík Bike Tours (p76) in the Old Harbour, or **Örninn** (⌨ 588 9890; www.orninn.is; Faxafen 8; ⊙10am-6pm Mon-Fri, 11am-3pm Sat) in southeast Reykjavík. The **Bike Cave** (Map p74; ⌨ 770 3113; www.facebook.com/bikecavereykjavik; Einarsnes 36; ⊙9am-10pm, shorter hours in winter; 🖳12), near Reykjavík Domestic Airport, can help with repairs.

BUS

Strætó (⌨ 540 2700; www.straeto.is) operates regular buses around Reykjavík and its suburbs (Seltjarnarnes, Kópavogur, Garðabær, Hafnarfjörður and Mosfellsbær); it also operates long-distance buses. It has online schedules, a smartphone app and a printed map. Many free maps like *Welcome to Reykjavík City Map* also include bus-route maps.

Buses run from 7am until 11pm or midnight daily (from 11am on Sunday). Services depart at 15-minute or 30-minute intervals. A limited night-bus service runs until 4.30am on Friday and Saturday. Buses only stop at designated bus stops, marked with a yellow letter 'S'.

The fare is 460kr; you can buy tickets at the bus terminal, on board (though no change is given) or by using the Strætó app. Buy one-/three-day passes (1700/4000kr) at Mjódd bus terminal, the Main Tourist Office, 10-11 convenience stores, many hotels, Kringlan and Smáralind shopping malls, and bigger swimming pools. If you need to take two buses to reach your destination, get a *skiptimiði* (transfer ticket) from the driver; it's good for 75 minutes in the city, 120 minutes in the countryside.

The Reykjavík City Card also acts as a Strætó bus pass.

TAXI

Taxi prices are high. Flagfall starts at around 700kr. Tipping is not required. From BSÍ bus terminal to Harpa concert hall costs about 2200kr. From Mjódd bus termimal it's about 4300kr.

There are usually taxis outside bus stations, airports and bars on weekend nights (huge queues for the bars), plus on Bankastræti near Lækjargata.

BSR (⌨ 561 0000; www.taxireykjavik.is)
Hreyfill (⌨ 588 5522; www.hreyfill.is)

Around the Ring Road

The Golden Circle

The Golden Circle takes in three popular attractions within 100km of the capital: Þingvellir, where tectonic plates meet; Geysir, where water erupts more than 100 times a day; and the roaring and staggeringly voluminous waterfall Gullfoss.

Þingvellir National Park (p22)

Sights

Ljósafoss Power Station MUSEUM
(Ljósafossstöð; ☎896 7407; www.landsvirkjun.com; Ljósafoss; ⏲10am-5pm Jun-Aug, shorter hours Sep-May) FREE The 1937 Ljósafoss Power Station catches the outflow of lake Úlfljótsvatn and turns it into electricity. In 2016, an elaborate state-of-the-art multimedia exhibition called Powering the Future opened, bringing the principles of electricity, hydropower, and geothermal and renewable energy to life.

Sleeping & Eating

There is a small **cafe** (grilled sandwiches from 400kr; ⏲9am-10pm Apr-Oct, shorter hours Nov-Mar) with a mini-mart at the Þingvellir Information Centre, serving sandwiches, hot dogs and soup, but the closest proper restaurant is at Ion Adventure Hotel. Otherwise bring your own food.

Ljósafossskóli Hostel GUESTHOUSE $
(☎699 2720; www.ljosafossskoli.is; Brúarási 1, Ljósafossskóli; d without bathroom from 10,500kr; P 📶) Many of the good, simple rooms in this modern, converted schoolhouse have excellent lake and mountain views. A particularly unusual feature is the full-sized sports hall (with basketball hoops) on the ground floor, which guests are free to use. Breakfast is 1500kr. Find it 28km south of Þingvellir and 21km north of Selfoss, on the edge of Úlfljótsvatn lake.

Útilífsmiðstöð Skáta Úlfljótsvatni CAMPGROUND $
(☎482 2674; www.ulfljotsvatn.is; off Rte 360, Úlfljótsvatn; sites per adult/child 1600kr/free, dm incl breakfast 4400kr; P 📶 🏊) This scouts centre has camping in summer and basic dorm huts in winter. It offers a full program of lakefront activities and extensive playgrounds. Find it on the southern side of Þingvellir's lake, Þingvallavatn. There's a small camp shop on-site.

RING ROAD SIGHTS

Coverage of the top sights in the towns and regions listed in this chapter can be found in the Road Trips chapters, along with information about driving between sights and towns.

Ion Adventure Hotel BOUTIQUE HOTEL **$$$**
(☑ 482 3415; www.ioniceland.is; Nesjavellir 801; d from 44,000kr; P@🛜🏊) 🅿 Ion is hip, ultra modern and remote. Using sustainable practices throughout, it has a geothermal pool, organic spa, and a **restaurant** (mains lunch 2600-4500kr, dinner 4000-12,000kr, 3-course dinner from 9900kr; ⏰ 11.30am-10pm) with slow-food local ingredients. The uber-cool bar has designer cardboard lampshades and floor-to-ceiling windows for Northern Lights watching. Rooms are a tad small, but kitted out impeccably.

ℹ Information

Þingvellir Information Centre (Leirar Þjónustumiðstöð; www.thingvellir.is; Rte 36; ⏰ 9am-10pm May-Aug, to 6pm Sep-Apr) On the northern side of the lake, this is a larger information centre with plenty of helpful info, plus a cafe and small store.

Þingvellir Visitor Centre (Gestastofa; ☑ 482 3613; off Rte 36; ⏰ 9am-7pm Jun-Aug, to 6.30pm Sep-May) Sitting above the Almannagjá rift is a basic visitor centre with restrooms (200kr per visit).

Laugarvatn (p23)

Laugarvatn HI Hostel HOSTEL **$**
(☑ 486 1215; www.laugarvatnhostel.is; Laugarvatns-vegur; dm/d without bathroom 5100/9900kr, d/t/q 14,200/16,100/20,300kr; ⏰ Feb-Nov; P@🛜🏊) This large, clean and friendly hostel is housed in a renovated two-storey building with plenty of kitchen space (great lake views while washing up or from the dining room). There's also a pool table, bar and breakfast buffet (for an additional 1500kr), plus a room discount for HI members.

★ Héraðsskólinn HOSTEL, GUESTHOUSE **$$**
(☑ 537 8060; www.heradsskolinn.is; 840 Laugarvatn; dm/d/q without bathroom from 4700/11,100/23,000kr, d with bathroom 18,500kr; P🛜) A beautifully unique lakeside boutique (originally built in 1928 by Guðjón Samúelsson) identifiable by its distinctive peaked green roofs. The interiors are sleek retro, with subtle nods to its old schoolhouse days. Design features include wooden desks, vintage maps and '50s-style chairs. It offers both private rooms with shared bathrooms (some sleep up to six) and dorms.

Good Burger BURGERS **$**
(☑ 666 1234; Dalbraut 6; burgers from 1100kr; ⏰ 11am-9pm) Serving the best burgers for miles, this simple joint has only four types

WORTH A TRIP

HALLDÓR LAXNESS' HOUSE

Nobel Prize–winning author Halldór Laxness (1902–98) lived in Mosfellsbær all his life. His riverside home is now the **Gljúfrasteinn Laxness Museum** (☑ 586 8066; www.gljufrasteinn.is; Þingvallavegur, Mosfellsbær; adult/child 900kr/free; ⏰ 9am-5pm Jun-Aug, 10am-4pm Tue-Sun Sep-May), easy to visit on the road from Reykjavík to Þingvellir (Rte 36). The author built this upper-class 1950s house and it remains intact with original furniture, writing room and Laxness' fine-art collection. An audio tour leads you round. Look for his beloved Jaguar parked out the front.

of flavoursome beef patties. Choose them small, medium or large (like really large!). The Aruba burger (with an onion ring on top of the patty) is our choice. Veggies, bacon, cheese, Béarnaise sauce and fries can be ordered as extras. Get Boli beer and soda on tap.

Geysir (p24)

Gljasteinn Skálinn CABIN, GUESTHOUSE **$**
(☑ 486 8757; www.gljasteinn.is; Myrkholt; dm adult/child 6500/4000kr, d without bathroom 11,000kr; 🛜) This beautiful farm in the widening sweep of the valley between Geysir and Gullfoss has a clutch of tidy houses, one of which has sleeping-bag accommodation dorms (four beds each) and doubles with shared bathrooms, plus a kitchen and living room. It also has cabins with dorm beds in the highlands on the Kjölur route (F35).

★ Hótel Geysir HOTEL **$$**
(☑ 480 6800; www.hotelgeysir.is; Biskupstungnabraut; s/d incl breakfast from 18,000/22,900kr; P@🛜) This four-star, 77-room hotel is minimalist cool. The facade has an entirely wooden front with only a small single doorway, which opens into a grand lobby, and the relics of the walls from the original building – once a Glima (Scandinavian martial art used by the Vikings) training facility. B&W photography of historic athletes decorates the walls. There's a restaurant serving a daily buffet (4200kr) from noon until late. At the time of writing, a new spa was being planned. It's located next to the Geysir Center.

Golden Circle

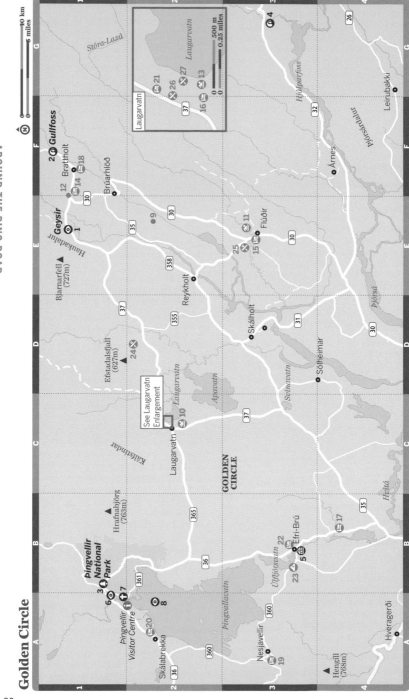

Golden Circle

◎ **Top Sights**

◎ **Sights**

⊕ **Activities, Courses & Tours**

🛏 **Sleeping**

🍴 **Eating**

🛍 **Shopping**

ℹ️ **Information**

Gullfoss (p24)

Hótel Gullfoss HOTEL **$$**

(☑486 8979; www.hotelgullfoss.is; Brattholt; d incl breakfast 20,000kr; 🛜) A few kilometres south of the falls, Hótel Gullfoss is a stylish bunga-low hotel. Its clean en suite rooms overlook the moors (get one facing the valley) and all have tea-and-coffee-making facilities and private bathrooms. There are two hot-pots and an on-site restaurant (mains 2500kr to 4900kr) with sweeping views.

Tourist Information Centre CAFE **$**

(www.gullfoss.is; Kjalvegur/Rte 35; menu items from 990kr; ⊗9am-9pm Jun-Aug, to 6.30pm Sep-May; 🛜) Above Gullfoss, the small tourist information centre boasts a large souvenir shop and a cafe serving coffee and a good selection of soups, salads, sandwiches and cakes.

Flúðir (p25)

Grund – Guesthouse Flúðir GUESTHOUSE **$$**

(Gistiheimilið Flúðum; ☑565 9196; www.gisting fludir.is; Skeiða-og Hrunamannavegur/Rte 30; d with/without bathroom incl breakfast 16,000/22,000kr; 🅿🛜) This adorable guesthouse has five cosy rooms filled with antiques, and a wing of modern rooms with private

bathrooms and decks with mountain views. The popular **restaurant** (mains 2000-4900kr; ⊗12.30pm-9pm Jun–mid-Aug, hours may vary) prides itself on offering fresh local food.

Hvolsvöllur & Around (p26)

Midgard Base Camp HOSTEL **$$**

(☑578 3180; www.midgard.is; Dufþaksbraut 14; dm/d from 5300/23,300kr; 🅿🛜) Smart bunk beds, crafted by local iron smiths, in dorms of four to six. Private rooms have fabulous views, also enjoyed from the communal rooftop with hot tub and sauna. Downstairs there's foosball and a comfy lounge area, plus a restaurant offering hearty meals that hit the spot after a day of outdoor adventures. The highland tours (p27) run from here get glowing reviews.

Spói Guesthouse B&B **$$**

(☑861 8687; www.spoiguesthouse.is; Hlíðarvegur 15/Rte 261; s/d without bathroom 13,200/18,900kr; 🅿🛜) This impeccable family-run guest-house has a collection of pristine rooms grouped around a large dining room with a broad wooden table where a lavish breakfast is served. The owners offer a wealth of local knowledge.

Skógar (p29)

⭐ **Skógar Campsite** CAMPGROUND $
(Skógafossvegur, near Rte 1; sites per person 1500kr; ☺ May-Sep) Basic grassy lot in a superb location, right next to Skógafoss. The sound of falling water makes a soothing lullaby to drift off to. There's a no-frills toilet and shower (300kr per person) block, plus a couple of washbasins for pots and pans. Pay at the small office window next to the showers.

⭐ **Skógar Guesthouse** GUESTHOUSE $$
(☑ 894 5464; www.skogarguesthouse.is; Ytri Skógar, off Skógaveur; d/tr without bathroom incl breakfast 23,800/35,700kr; 🛜) This charming white farmhouse is tucked in a strand of trees, beyond the Hótel Edda, almost to the cliff face. A friendly family offers quaint, impeccably maintained rooms with crisp linens and cosy quilts, and a large immaculate kitchen. A hot tub on a wood deck sits beneath the maples. It feels out of the tourist fray, despite being just a 10-minute walk from Skógafoss.

Hótel Skógafoss HOTEL $$
(☑ 487 8780; www.hotelskogafoss.is; Skógafossvegur, off Rte 1; d incl breakfast 27,200-29,500kr; 🛜) Nineteen well-put-together, modern rooms (half of which have views of Skógafoss) and good bathrooms. There's a well-located **bistro-bar** (mains 1900-3300kr; ☺ 11am-9pm), with plate-glass windows looking onto the falls, and local beer on tap.

Hótel Skógar HOTEL $$$
(☑ 487 4880; www.hotelskogar.is; Skógarfossvegur, near Rte 1; s/d/tr incl breakfast 24,300/27,600/34,100kr; 🛜) This architecturally interesting hotel has 12 small, eclectic rooms with quirky antiques, some with hill views. From the garden you can see Eyjafjöll glacier and the Skógafoss waterfall. A hot tub and sauna plus an elegant **restaurant** (mains 1600kr to 4900kr; ☺ noon to 3pm and 6pm to 10pm) round it out. Good breakfast too.

Vík (p29)

🛏 Sleeping

⭐ **Vík HI Hostel** HOSTEL $
(Norður-Vík Hostel; ☑ 487 1106; www.hostel.is; Suðurvíkurvegur 5; dm/s/d incl breakfast without bathroom 6500/10,200/18,000kr, cottages from 40,000kr; @🛜) 🏴 Vík's small, cosy, year-round hostel is in the beige house on the hill behind the village centre. Good facilities include a guest kitchen, and several stand-

alone cottages sleep up to eight people. Staff can arrange local tours like zip-lining and paragliding (May to September, 14,900kr and 35,000kr). There's a discount for HI members. Green-certified.

Vík Campsite CAMPGROUND $
(Tjaldsvæðið Vík; ☑ 487 1345; www.vikcamping. is; Klettsvegur 7; sites per adult/child 1750kr/free; ☺ Jun-Sep; P🛜) The campsite sits under a grassy ridge at the eastern end of town, just beyond the Icelandair Hótel Vík. An octagonal building houses cooking facilities, a washing machine, toilets and showers (200kr) and laundry services (500kr). There are also four little cottages (25,000kr).

⭐ **Guesthouse Carina** B&B $$
(☑ 699 0961; www.guesthousecarina.is; Mýrarbraut 13, off Rte 1; s/d without bathroom from 16,900/21,900/25,900kr; P🛜) Friendly Carina and her husband Ingvar run one of the best lodging options in Vík. Neat-as-a-pin, spacious rooms with good light and clean shared bathrooms fill a large converted house near the centre of town.

⭐ **Icelandair Hótel Vík** HOTEL $$$
(☑ 487 1480, bookings 444 4000; www.icelandairhotels.com; Klettsvegur 1-5; d economy/regular from 22,000/45,000kr; P🛜) This sleek black-window-fronted hotel has merged with the former next-door Hótel Edda. It sits on the eastern edge of town with 88 rooms, some suitably swanky, while the former Hótel Edda rooms are still modern but an economical option. Choose from views to the rear cliffs or the sea. The light, natural decor is inspired by the local environment. Breakfast costs 3000kr.

🍴 Eating & Drinking

Ice Cave Restaurant INTERNATIONAL $
(☑ 788 5070; Austurvegur, Rte 1; mains from 1450kr; ☺ 11am-9pm) This modern canteen-style dining room has futuristic lighting (with electric tree-like centrepieces) and serves surprisingly satisfying deli-style food from trays. Pick from sandwiches, salads, noodles, marinated chicken legs, lamb chops, chicken curry and burgers.

⭐ **Suður-Vík** ICELANDIC, ASIAN $$
(☑ 487 1515; www.facebook.com/Sudurvik; Suðurvíkurvegur 1; mains 1300-5350kr; ☺ noon-10pm, shorter hours in winter) The friendly ambience, in a warmly lit building with hardwood floors, exposed beams and interesting artwork, helps to elevate this restaurant beyond its compe-

tition. Food is Icelandic hearty, ranging from farm plates and quinoa salad with chicken to pizzas and Asian dishes (think spicy Panang curry with rice). Book ahead in summer. For an nightcap head to the **Man Cave** (beers from 1000kr; ☺6pm-late) downstairs.

Smiðjan Brugghús MICROBREWERY (http://smidjanbrugghus.is; Sunnubraut 15; ☺11.30am-midnight Sun-Thu, to 1am Fri & Sat) Vík's hippest hang-out is warehouse-style with grey walls, windows looking onto the brewing room and blackboards displaying 10 craft beers on tap. Hop aficionados can try Icelandic India Pale Ales, pale ale, porter and farmhouse ale with a handful of different burgers (including a vegan patty).

ℹ Information

Tourist Information Centre (☑487 1395; www.kotlusetur.i; Víkurbraut 28; ☺10am-8pm May-Sep, noon-6pm Oct-Apr; ☎) Inside the museum **Brydebúð** (adult/child 500kr/free; ☺10am-6pm Mon-Fri, noon-7pm Sat & Sun Jun-Aug). Has friendly advice about the local area, maps, books and a small gift shop.

Kirkjubæjarklaustur (Klauster; p33)

Iceland Bike Farm MOUNTAIN BIKING (☑692 6131; www.icelandbikefarm.is; Mörtunga II) This new company is run by a young farming couple who are passionate about their surrounds. Tours are on fatbikes (off-road bicycles with oversized tyres) that are perfect for the Icelandic conditions (snow, mud, sand) and enable year-round tours. There's a half-/full-day single-track expedition (15,000/25,000kr), plus some great two-day activity tours (from 100,000kr) in summer, including one that heads to Skaftafell.

Some tours operate year-round, and pick up in Klaustur is possible. The website outlines what experience is required for each tour, and what is included.

Home base is the farm at the end of Rte 202, northeast of Klaustur, where there is glamping (glamorous camping) for tour participants.

Kirkjubær II CAMPGROUND $ (☑894 4495; www.kirkjubaer.com; sites per person 1400kr, cottages 19,000-21,000kr) A neat green site with sheltering hedges, right in town. Good service buildings include kitchen, showers and laundry. A boon in bad weather; there's seven basic heated huts, each

sleeping four in bunk beds (BYO sleeping bag). Each cottage has either a toilet or a kitchenette.

Hörgsland COTTAGES, GUESTHOUSE $$ (☑487 6655; www.horgsland.is; sites per person 1600kr, cottages for 2/6 from 24,800/39,000kr, d/q with bathroom incl breakfast 24,700/34,400kr; ☎) On the Ring Road about 8km north-east of Klaustur is this mini village of 13 spotless, spacious, self-contained cottages that can sleep six (note: on the website, these cottages are called 'guesthouses'). A recent addition is a block of spick-and-span rooms, with and without bathroom. There's also camping, plus outdoor hot-pots, and a simple shop and cafe.

★**Magma Hotel** BOUTIQUE HOTEL $$$ (☑420 0800; www.magmahotel.is; d incl breakfast from 43,000kr; ☎) Winning hearts with its beautiful design, peaceful surrounds and friendly staff, this intimate new hotel is a gem. It's just a few kilometres out of Klaustur on Rte 204, by a lake and looking onto lush views. Individual turf-roofed chalets (named for volcanoes) are an ode to good taste, and each features a fridge, coffee machine and bluetooth speaker, plus a patio. There's a stylish on-site bistro for guests.

ℹ Information

Skaftárstofa Visitor Centre (☑487 4620; www.visitklaustur.is; Klausturvegur 10; ☺9am-6pm mid-Jun–mid-Sep, to 5pm mid-May–mid-Jun, 9am-2pm Mon-Fri mid-Sep–mid-May) The helpful tourist office is inside the Skaftárstofa Visitor Centre, with good local info plus coverage and exhibitions on Katla Geopark and Vatnajökull National Park – this is the base for the lesser-visited western pocket of the national park, only accessible by 4WD or bus. There's also a short film on the Laki eruption.

Lómagnúpur & Around (p33)

★**Dalshöfði Guesthouse** GUESTHOUSE $$ (☑487 4781; http://dalshofdi.is; d/f without bathroom incl breakfast 21,090/33,250kr) An appealing option in this area is Dalshöfði Guesthouse, in a remote and scenic farm setting 5km north of the Ring Road. Rooms are bright and spotless, with access to a kitchen and a sunny, plant-filled outdoor deck. There's a two-bedroom apartment here (37,050kr) too, and some lovely hiking trails in the area.

South Coast

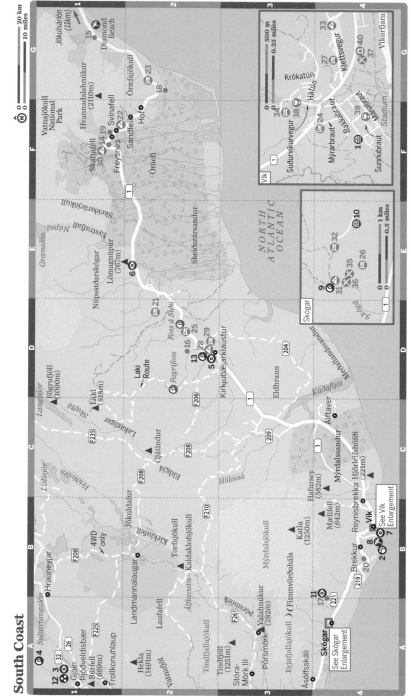

South Coast

Skaftafell (p34)

⊙ Tours

★ **Local Guide**   ADVENTURE
(☑894 1317; www.localguide.is; Freysnes) Local Guide is a family-owned business – the family has lived in the area for generations, so local knowledge is first-rate. Tours depart from the petrol station in Freysnes, about 5km from Skaftafell. From here, guides run year-round glacier hikes and ice climbs; the shortest tour offers one hour on the ice for adult/child 9490/8900kr (minimum age 10). Local Guide is also a long-standing expert on ice caves, and runs tours from mid-November to March. The standard ice-cave tour costs 19,900kr, but there are longer tours, plus options for private tours to more remote caves. The website outlines all the details.

Atlantsflug   SCENIC FLIGHTS
(☑854 4105; www.flightseeing.is; ⊙May-Sep) Sightseeing flights offer a brilliant perspective over all this natural splendour, and leave from the tiny airfield on the Ring Road, just by the turn-off to the Skaftafellsstofa Visitor Centre. Choose between seven options, with views over Landmannalaugar, Lakagígar, Skaftafell peaks, Jökulsárlón and Grímsvötn. Prices start from 26,100kr for 20 minutes on the 'pilot special' surprise route (determined by weather and conditions). Off-season flights are possible by arrangement.

Icelandic Mountain Guides   ADVENTURE
(IMG; ☑Reykjavík 587 9999, Skaftafell 894 2959; www.mountainguides.is) IMG's best-selling walk is the family-friendly 'Blue Ice Experience', with 1½ to two hours spent on the ice (adult/child 10,900/7900kr, minimum age eight years). These tours run from Skaftafell four to eight times daily year-round. There are longer three-hour walks up the same glacier (16,900kr), and an option to combine with an introduction to ice climbing (19,900kr).

⊟ Sleeping

Skaftafell Campsite   CAMPGROUND $
(☑470 8300; www.vjp.is; sites per adult/teen/child 1400/800kr/free; 🛜) Most visitors bring a tent (or campervan) to this large, gravelly, pano-

ramic campsite (with laundry facilities, and hot showers for 500kr). It gets very busy in summer, with a capacity of 400 pitches; note that the site is open year-round. Reservations are only required for large groups (40-plus people). No cooking facilities are provided. Wi-fi is available in the visitor centre.

If you're looking for a less crowded option, consider the **campground** ([phone] 478 1765; www. svinafell.com; sites per person 1700kr, r & cabins per person 4500-5200kr; [calendar] campground May-Sep; [wifi]) at Svínafell, 8km east.

ℹ Information

Skaftafellsstofa Visitor Centre ([phone] 470 8300; www.vjp.is; [calendar] 8am-7pm Jun-Sep, 9am-6pm Feb-May & Oct, 10am-6pm Nov-Jan; [wifi]) The helpful year-round visitor centre has an information desk plus maps for sale, informative exhibitions, a summertime cafe and internet access. The staff here know their stuff, and are keen to impart knowledge and help you prepare for hiking.

Ingólfshöfði (p35)

Fosshotel Glacier Lagoon HOTEL **$$$**
([phone] 514 8300; www.fosshotel.is; Hnappavellir; r from 39,000kr; [wifi]) The name is misleading: this large new four-star hotel sits halfway between Skaftafell and Jökulsárlón at Hnappavellir, about 3km east of the departure point for Ingólfshöfði tours. There are *no* lagoon views – Jökulsárlón is a 20-minute drive away. Opened in 2016, the hotel houses 104 simple but stylish rooms (with more under construction), plus a good restaurant and inviting bar area. The restaurant (dinner mains 4180kr to 6990kr) offers high-quality local produce; there's also a more reasonably priced all-day bar menu. The hotel's prices are steep but demand in this region is sky-high, so it pays to book early.

Hali to Höfn (p38)

Glacier Adventure ADVENTURE
([phone] 571 4577; www.glacieradventures.is; Hali) The closest guiding company to Jökulsárlón is locally owned Glacier Adventure, based 13km east of the lagoon, operating from **Hali Country Hotel** ([phone] 478 1073; www.hali.is; s/d/apt incl breakfast 28,500/36,500/51,900kr; [wifi]). Glacier walks are done on Breiðamerkurjökull, with one to 1½ hours on the ice (adult/child 14,900/7450kr). Half-day ice-climbing excursions (24,900kr) and winter ice-cave visits (from 19,500kr), including a challenging option to a more remote cave, are also available.

★ **Guesthouse Skálafell** GUESTHOUSE **$$**
([phone] 478 1041; www.skalafell.net; d with/without bathroom incl breakfast 28,500/24,150kr, cottage 38,500kr; [wifi]) At the foot of Skálafellsjökull, this friendly working farm has a handful of agreeable rooms in the family farmhouse, and also in motel-style units and family-sized cottages. There are no cooking facilities, but dinner is available. In cooperation with the national park, the knowledgeable owners offer information and have set up marked **walking trails** (open to all) in the surrounding glaciated landscapes.

★ **Jón Ríki** ICELANDIC **$$**
([phone] 478 2063; www.jonriki.is; mains 2600-5900kr; [calendar] 5-9.30pm) This fabulous farmhouse restaurant at Hólmur (p43) is something of a surprise, with funky decor, a small in-house brewery, and beautifully presented, high-quality dishes: grilled langoustine, avocado chips and panna cotta for dessert. Sourdough pizza also gets a mention – it goes well with super-interesting house brews like the mango IPA or the jalapeno-and-pumpkin ale. It can get busy, so a reservation is advised.

Höfn (p39)

✦ Festivals & Events

Humarhátíð FOOD & DRINK
Every year in late June or early July, Höfn's langoustine festival honours this tasty crustacean, hauled to shore in abundance by the local fishing fleet. There's usually a fun fair, dancing, music, lots of alcohol and even a few langoustines.

⌁ Sleeping

Höfn Camping & Cottages CAMPGROUND **$**
([phone] 478 1606; www.campsite.is; Hafnarbraut 52; campsite per person 1800kr, d cottage excl linen 12,000kr) Lots of travellers stay at the campground on the main road into town. There are 11 decent-value cottages, sleeping up to six; some have private toilet, but all use the amenities block for showers. There's a playground and laundry, and some camping gear is sold at the reception. The downsides: very few showers for the capacity, and no wi-fi.

★ **Milk Factory** GUESTHOUSE **$$$**
([phone] 478 8900; www.milkfactory.is; Dalbraut 2; d/q incl breakfast 30,000/39,500kr; [wifi]) Full credit to the family – and the designers – behind the restoration of this old dairy factory

north of town. There are 17 modern, hotel-standard rooms here, including two with disabled access. The prize allotments are the six spacious mezzanine suites that sleep four – good for families or friends, although they don't have kitchens.

★ **Old Airline Guesthouse**   GUESTHOUSE $$
(☑478 1300; www.oldairline.com; Hafnarbraut 24; s/d without bathroom incl breakfast 16,500/21,700kr; ☜) This central guesthouse sparkles under the care of friendly host Sigga. On offer are five fresh rooms with shared bathrooms, plus a large lounge and guest kitchen (with self-service breakfast). Big brownie points to free laundry access. It's attached to a small electronics/IT store.

✖ Eating

Otto Matur & Drykkur   ICELANDIC $$
(☑478 1818; Hafnarbraut 2; mains 2890-5990kr; ☺noon-10pm) A new incarnation for the oldest house in Höfn (dating from 1897) has turned it into an elegant space high on Nordic style. The small menu spotlights fresh local produce – langoustine is here, of course, as well as simple, elegant dishes of salmon, lamb and more. There's also a cool little bar in the cellar (open until 1am).

❶ Information

Gamlabúð Visitor Centre (☑470 8330; www.visitvatnajokull.is; Heppuvegur 1; ☺9am-7pm Jun-Aug, to 6pm May & Sep, to 5pm Oct-Apr) Harbourfront Gamlabúð houses a national-park visitor centre with excellent exhibits, local tourist information and maps for sale. Ask about activities and hiking trails in the area.

Djúpivogur (p43)

★ **Bragðavellir Cottages**   COTTAGE $$
(☑787 2121; www.bragdavellir.is; 1-/2-bedroom cottage 25,000/36,000kr; ☜) Some 13km from Djúpivogur, this pristine property is rich in views and wildlife (including ducks and chickens; possibly reindeer in winter), and there are great walking trails. A cluster of cosy self-contained cottages come in two sizes – one or two bedroom. There's an on-site 'barn restaurant', too.

❶ Information

Information Centre (☑470 8740; ☺9am-5pm Mon-Fri, 10am-2pm Sat & Sun mid-May–mid-Sep) The town's seasonal information centre is at the entrance to the campground.

Breiðdalsvík (p44)

Hótel Bláfell   HOTEL $$
(☑470 0000; www.hotelblafell.is; Sólvellir 14; s/d incl breakfast from 12,800/17,100; ☜) Located in the centre of 'town' (we use that term lightly), Hótel Bláfell has smart monochrome rooms (some timber-lined), a sauna and a superb guest lounge with open fire. The hotel also has quality two-bedroom apartments in town, and owns Hotel Post next door. Campers will find a small **campsite** (sites per person kr1000; ☺May-Sep) behind the hotel.

Egilsstaðir & Around (p47)

Tehúsið Hostel   HOSTEL $
(☑471 2450; www.tehusidhostel.is; Kaupvangur 17; dm/d without bathroom from 6850/19,000kr; ☜) A welcome addition to the local scene, the Teahouse has six bunk-filled rooms – the spaces are tight, but the price is reasonable (rooms can be booked as doubles or family rooms). There's a communal kitchen, but the best feature is the chilled cafe-bar, filled with character and a fine place to relax over a beer. Breakfast is served here (open to all, including the campers from next door's campground) from 1500kr; of an evening, try drinks like such as the bramble gin or rhubarb mojito.

Hótel Eyvindará   HOTEL, COTTAGES $$
(☑471 1200; www.eyvindara.is; Eyvindará II; s/d incl breakfast from 21,900/25,200kr; ☺Apr-Nov; ☜) Set 3km out of town (on Rte 94), Eyvindará is a handsome, family-run collection of new hotel rooms, plus good motel-style units and cute timber cottages. The cottages sit hidden among fir trees, while motel rooms enjoy verandahs and views. It's known for friendly staff, and there's a decent restaurant (open June to August) and a stylish lounge area, plus new hot-pots.

**Gistihúsið – Lake
Hotel Egilsstaðir**   HOTEL $$$
(☑471 1114; www.lakehotel.is; Egilsstöðum 1-2; d incl breakfast from 29,400kr; @☜) The town was named after this farm and splendid heritage guesthouse (now big enough to warrant the 'hotel' label) on the banks of Lagarfljót, 300m west of the crossroads. In its old wing, en-suite rooms retain a sense of character. In contrast, a new extension houses 30 modern, slightly anonymous rooms. There's a great restaurant (p98) on-site, and a **spa** (hotel guest/nonguest 2000/3500kr; ☺10am-10pm).

★**Eldhúsið** ICELANDIC **$$$**
(📞471 1114; www.lakehotel.is; Egilsstöðum 1-2; lunch 1490-3990kr, dinner mains 3390-64390kr; ⊘11.30am-10pm; 🖥📶) Some of the east's most creative cooking happens at the restaurant inside Gistihúsið – Lake Hotel Egilsstaðir (p97). The menu is an ode to locally sourced produce (lamb, fish and game), and the speciality is the beef, raised right here on the farm. Try a rib-eye with Béarnaise, or fjord-fresh fish with grape salad and dill mayonnaise. Desserts are pretty, polished affairs. Bookings advised. The chef's three-course menu of farm produce costs 9190kr and represents good value for the high standard offered. Note: vegan choices, too.

ℹ Information

Egilsstaðastofa Visitor Center (📞470 0750; www.visitegilsstadir.is; Kaupvangur 17; ⊘7am-11pm Jun-Aug, 8am-3pm Mon-Fri May & Sep, 8am-noon Mon-Fri Oct-Apr; 📶) From its info desk at the campground reception, this place focuses on Egilsstaðir and surrounds and can hook you up with bus tickets and various activity tours: hiking, super-Jeep tours, sea-angling etc. Bike hire is available (2000kr for up to four hours, 3000kr for 24 hours).

Snæfellsstofa – National Park Visitor Centre (📞470 0840; www.vjp.is; ⊘9am-5pm Jun-Aug, 10am-3pm May & Sep) This stylish centre covers the eastern territory of Vatnajökull National Park. Displays highlight the nature of Snæfell mountain and the eastern highlands, and staff sell maps and offer advice to travellers wishing to hike or otherwise experience the park.

Mývatn & Around (p55)

Mývatn lake is circled by a 36km sealed road. The main settlement is Reykjahlíð, in the northeast corner - an information centre is here, as are most sleeping and eating options.

⊙ Sights & Activities

★**Lofthellir** CAVE
The dramatic lava cave at Lofthellir is a stunning destination, with magnificent natural ice sculptures dominating the interior. Although it's one of Mývatn's highlights, the cave is on private property and can only be accessed on a half-day tour with Geo Travel. The tour involves a one-hour 4WD journey and a 25-minute walk across gorgeous lava fields to reach the cave, and then the donning of special equipment (headlamps, studded boots etc) and intensely physical

wriggling through tight spaces. Wear warm, waterproof gear. Winter tours cross snowfields. In summer, you can cycle to the cave with Mývatn Activity – Hike&Bike. While Geo Travel runs the tours, they can also be booked via **Saga Travel** (📞558 8888; www.sagatravel.is; Fjölnisgata 6a; ⊘booking office 8am-4pm Mon-Fri, to 2pm Sat & Sun).

★**Víti** VOLCANO
(Rte 863) The ochre crater of Víti reveals a secret when you reach its rim – a cerulean pool of floodwater at its heart. The 300m-wide explosion crater was created in 1724 at the beginning of the destructive Mývatn Fires. There is a circular path from the car park around the rim.

Note: don't confuse this Víti crater with the Víti crater beside the Askja caldera (you can bathe inside the latter, but not the former). Fun fact: Víti means 'hell' in Icelandic.

Vindbelgjarfjall HIKING
(Rte 1) The steep but relatively straightforward climb up 529m-high Vindbelgjarfjall (also known as Vindbelgur), on Mývatn lake's western shore, offers one of the best views across the lake and its alien pseudocraters. The trail to the summit starts at a car park south of the peak, near the farm Vagnbrekka. Reckon on at least a half-hour to reach the mount, and another half-hour to climb to the summit.

☞ Tours

★**Geo Travel** ADVENTURE TOUR
(📞464 4442; www.geotravel.is) A small company owned by two well-connected local guys who plant trees to carbon offset their tours. They offer excellent year-round small-group trips, from tours of lava and ice cave Lofthellir (17,500kr) to super-Jeep excursions to Askja and Holuhraun (34,900kr), Northern Lights tours (17,500kr) and half-hour snowmobile trips (14,900kr). They're also birdwatching specialists.

Mývatn Activity –
Hike&Bike ADVENTURE TOUR
(📞899 4845; www.hikeandbike.is) Hike&Bike has a booth by the Gamli Bærinn (p100) tavern in Reykjahlíð that offers tour bookings and mountain-bike rental (adult/child 5000/4000kr per day). A vast program of cycling and hiking tours includes a fat-bike ride to Lofthellir lava and ice cave (24,900kr), a one-hour ATV-ride (22,500kr)

Mývatn & Krafla

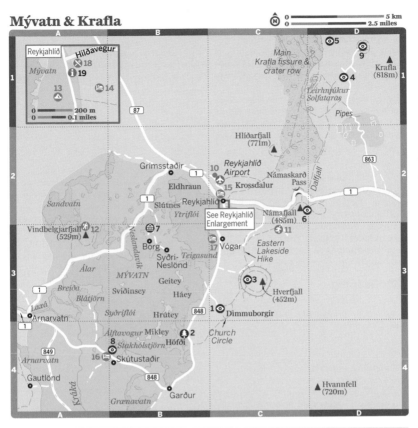

Mývatn & Krafla

and an evening sightseeing cycle that ends with a soak at the nature baths (p53; including baths admission 13,500kr). The company shines in its local network and knowledge, and in the winter pursuits it

can arrange (dog sledding, snowshoeing around Dimmuborgir, cross-country skiing and snowmobiling on the frozen lake). It can put together packages that cover accommodation.

Snowdogs
DOG SLEDDING

($847 7199; www.snowdogs.is; off Rte 849; sled tour adult/child 30,000/10,000kr) Sæmi and his family run winter dog-sledding tours across snow-white wilderness on remote farm Heiði, about 8km off Rte 848 in southern Mývatn (take Rte 849 west of Skútustaðir). Tours vary depending on the dogs, people, weather and trail conditions, but guests are generally on the snow for 45 to 60 minutes and cover around 8km. Dog cart rides in summer cost 19,000kr. Kennel visits cost 3500kr.

Mýflug Air
SCENIC FLIGHT

($464 4400; www.myflug.is; Reykjahlíð Airport) Mýflug Air operates daily flightseeing excursions (weather permitting) including a 20-minute trip over Mývatn and Krafla (19,000kr). A two-hour 'super tour' (57,000kr) also includes Dettifoss, Ásbyrgi, Kverkfjöll, Herðubreið and Askja. Or fly north for a one-hour stop in Grímsey (48,000kr).

🛏 Sleeping

Accommodation everywhere in the Mývatn area is in strong demand, and prices reflect this. Book ahead.

Bjarg
CAMPGROUND $

($464 4240; ferdabjarg@simnet.is; Rte 1; site per person 2000kr; ⊙mid-May–Sep) This campsite has a gorgeous, peaceful location on the Reykjahlíð lakeshore (though it gets packed and noisy in summer) almost opposite the supermarket ($464 4466; www.samkaup.is; ⊙9am-7pm Mon-Fri, 10am-6pm Sat, noon-6pm Sun). There is a cooking area (no stoves or utensils, so bring everything), laundry service (1200kr per wash or dry), tour-booking desk and bike hire. Note: no wi-fi.

Vogafjós Guesthouse
GUESTHOUSE $$

($464 3800; www.vogafjos.net; Rte 1, Vógar; d incl breakfast from 25,600kr; 🛜) Fresh scents of pine and cedar fill the air in these log-cabin rooms (cosy with underfloor heating), set in a lava field 2.5km south of Reykjahlíð and a few minutes' walk from the Cowshed restaurant, where breakfast is served. Most rooms sleep two, with family rooms also available.

Helluhraun 13
B&B $$

($464 4132; www.helluhraun13.blogspot.com; Helluhraun 13; d without bathroom incl breakfast 19,000kr; ⊙Jun-Aug; 🛜) Ásdis is the sunny host at this small, homely guesthouse with lava-field views. There are just three rooms and one bathroom, but they're bright, spotless and tastefully decorated.

🍴 Eating

⭐ Vogafjós
ICELANDIC $$

($464 3800; www.vogafjos.net; Rte 848; dishes 2000-5900kr; ⊙10am-11pm Jun-Aug, shorter hours rest of year; 🛜🍴♿) The 'Cowshed', 2.5km south of Reykjahlíð, is a memorable restaurant where you can enjoy views of the lush surrounds, or of the dairy shed of this working farm (cows are milked at 7.30am and 5.30pm). The menu is an ode to local produce: smoked lamb, house-made mozzarella, dill-cured Arctic char, geysir bread, home-baked cakes and homemade ice cream. It's all delicious. The kitchen closes at 10pm in summer.

Gamli Bærinn
ICELANDIC $$

($464 4270; www.myvatnhotel.is; Rte 1; mains 2100-4000kr; ⊙10am-11pm; 🛜) The cheerfully busy 'Old Farm' tavern beside Hótel Reynihlíð serves up good-quality pub-style meals all day, ranging from lamb soup, burgers and grilled trout to pizzas. In the evening it becomes a local hang-out – opening hours may be extended at weekends, but the kitchen closes at 10pm.

ℹ Information

Mývatnsstofa Visitor Centre ($464 4390; www.visitmyvatn.is; Hraunvegur 8; ⊙8.30am-6pm Jun-Aug, shorter hours rest of year) This well-informed centre has good displays on local geology and park rangers to advise on local sights. Pick up a copy of the useful Mývatn map, which gives a decent overview of hiking trails in the area (though it's not to scale). All tours and buses leave from the car park here.

Akureyri (p57)

🏇 Activities & Tours

⭐ Skjaldarvík
HORSE RIDING, ADVENTURE TOUR

($552 5200; www.skjaldarvik.is; Rte 816; horse rides from 11,900kr, buggy tours s/d 23,900/38,800kr) Skjaldarvík offers a couple of top-notch activities from its scenic fjordside locale 6km north of town: horse-riding tours, plus fun adrenaline-pumping buggy rides. These buggies are golf carts on steroids; you'll drive along trails on the surrounding farm (driving licence required; helmet and overalls supplied). Their base has a superb guesthouse (s/d without bathroom incl breakfast 20,900/22,600kr; @🛜) and restaurant. Horse-riding tours (one hour) run along the fjord and into the surrounding hills.

You can combine these activities in a package that includes access to Skjaldarvík's outdoor hot-pot and a two-course dinner. Pickup in Akureyri included.

Hlíðarfjall Ski Centre
SKIING

(📞462 2280; www.hlidarfjall.is; Rte 837; day pass adult/child 4900/1400kr; 🚻) Iceland's premier downhill ski slope is 5km west of town. The resort has a vertical drop of 537m, and a recently added lift has increased the longest trail to over 2.6km. There are eight lifts, 23 alpine slopes and also cross-country ski routes.

The season usually runs from November to May, with best conditions in February and March (Easter is particularly busy). In the long hours of winter darkness, all of the main runs are floodlit.

There's ski and snowboard rental, two restaurants and a ski school. In season, buses usually connect the site with Akureyri; check the website for details and www.skiiceland.is for great passes.

🛏 Sleeping

Hamrar Campsite
CAMPGROUND $

(📞461 2264; www.hamrar.is; sites per person 1500kr; ⊙mid-May–late Sep) This huge site, 1.5km south of town in a leafy setting in Kjarnaskógur woods, has newer facilities than the **city campsite** (📞462 3379; www.hamrar.is; Þórunnarstræti 23; sites per adult 1500kr; ⊙early Jun–mid-Sep), and mountain views. There's a hostel-style building here that has the cheapest beds in town: mattresses on the floor in a sleeping loft for 2000kr.

Akureyri Backpackers
HOSTEL $

(📞571 9050; www.akureyribackpackers.com; Hafnarstræti 98; dm from 4900kr; d without bathroom 14,300kr; 🛜) Supremely placed in the town's heart, this backpackers has a chilled travellers' vibe and a popular bar. Rooms spread over three floors: four- to eight-bed dorms, plus private rooms (on the top floor). Minor gripe: there are toilets and sinks on all levels but showers are in the basement, as is the free sauna. There's a small kitchen and a laundry. Breakfast 1215kr.

★ Icelandair Hotel Akureyri
HOTEL $$

(📞518 1000; www.icelandairhotels.com; Þingvallastræti 23; d from 22,100kr; 🅿🛜) This high-class hotel showcases Icelandic designers and artists within its fresh, white-and-caramel-toned decor; rooms are compact but well designed. Added extras: outdoor terrace, good on-site restaurant, and a

lounge (high tea 2750kr; ⊙high tea 2-5pm) serving high tea in the afternoon and happy-hour cocktails in the early evening.

Guesthouse Hvítahúsið
GUESTHOUSE $$

(📞869 9890; www.guesthousenorth.is; Gilsbakkavegur 13; d without bathroom from 16,400kr; 🛜) In an elevated, hidden residential pocket behind Kaupvangsstræti, the 'White House' shines with the personal touch of its stylish owner, Guðrún. There are five rooms, plus a kitchen with free tea and coffee. (Note: no breakfast served.) Attic rooms are the pick – one has a balcony.

Hrafninn
GUESTHOUSE $$

(📞462 5600; www.hrafninn.is; Brekkugata 4; s/d from 20,000/24,700kr; 🛜) Branding itself as a 'boutique guesthouse', central Hrafninn (the Raven) feels like an elegant manor house without being pretentious or stuffy. Over three floors, all rooms have bathroom and TV; the common areas feature some cool artworks. There is a small communal kitchenette for guests. Note: no breakfast served.

★ Sæluhús
APARTMENT $$$

(📞412 0800; www.saeluhus.is; Sunnutröð; studio/house from 26,750/32,250kr; 🛜) This awesome mini-village of modern studios and houses is perfect for a few days' R&R. The houses may be better equipped than your own back home: three bedrooms (sleeping seven), kitchen, washing machine and verandah with hot tub and barbecue. Smaller studios are ideal for couples, with kitchen and access to a laundry (some have a hot tub, but these cost extra).

🍴 Eating

Kristjáns Bakarí
BAKERY, CAFE $

(Hafnarstræti 108; sandwiches 500-900kr; ⊙8am-5pm Mon-Fri, to 4.30pm Sat, 9am-4.30pm Sun) For a quick pit stop or for picnic supplies, this small bakery and cafe on the main drag sells breads, cakes and pastries.

Berlin
CAFE $

(📞772 5061; www.facebook.com/berlinakureyri; Skipagata 4; breakfast 800-1700kr; ⊙8am-6pm; 🛜🌱) Breakfast served all day? Hello Berlin! If you need a fix of bacon and eggs or avocado on toast, this cosy timber-lined cafe is your spot. Good coffee is a bonus, and you can linger over waffles with caramel sauce too. From 11.30am the menu adds lunch-y offerings such as vegetable dhal and chicken wings.

Akureyri

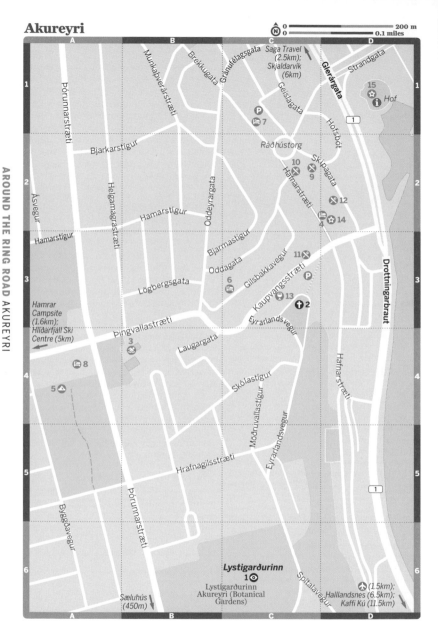

★ **Strikið** INTERNATIONAL $$
(📞 462 7100; www.strikid.is; Skipagata 14; mains lunch 2000-3200kr, dinner 4000-5500kr; ⏰ 11.30am-10pm) Huge windows with fjord views lend a magical glitz to this 5th-floor restaurant, and the cool cocktails help things along. The menu showcases prime Icelandic produce (reindeer burgers, superfresh sushi, lamb shoulder, shellfish soup). Crème brûlée makes for a sweet ending. The four-course signature menu is 9000kr. Reserve ahead.

Akureyri

Rub23   INTERNATIONAL $$$
(☑462 2223; www.rub23.is; Kaupvangsstræti 6;
mains lunch 2600-3200kr, dinner 5000-5900kr;
⊙11.30am-2pm & 5.30-10pm Mon-Fri, 5.30-10pm
Sat & Sun) This sleek, seafood-showcasing res-
taurant has a decidedly Japanese flavour, but
also promotes its use of 'rubs' or marinades
(along the lines of sweet mango chilli or citrus
rosemary). The food is first-rate, and at dinner
there's an array of menus (including a sushi
menu and tasting menus). Bookings advised.

🍷 Drinking & Nightlife

★**Ölstofa Akureyrar**   BAR
(☑663 8886; www.facebook.com/olstofak; Kaup-
vangsstræti 23; ⊙6pm-1am Mon-Thu, to 3am Fri &
Sat, to 10pm Sun) *The* place in town for draught
and local beers, this convivial spot has re-
cently partnered with local (and well-loved)
brewery Einstök to create a brewer's lounge
(www.brewerslounge.is) where you sample
their delicious wares, fresh from the brewery.

Akureyri Backpackers   BAR
(☑571 9050; www.akureyribackpackers.com; Hafnar-
stræti 98; ⊙reception 7.30am-11pm Sun-Thu, to 1am
Fri & Sat) Always a hub of convivial main-street
activity, the fun timber-clad bar at Akureyri
Backpackers (p101) is beloved of travellers and
locals for its occasional live music, good-value
burgers and weekend brunches, and a wide
beer selection – this is a fine spot to sample
local microbrews Kaldi and Einstök.

ⓘ Information

Tourist Office (☑450 1050; www.visitakureyri.
is; Hof, Strandgata 12; ⊙8am-6.30pm Jun–
mid-Sep, 8am-4pm Mon-Fri mid-Sep–Apr,
8am-4pm May; 🛜) This friendly, efficient office
is inside **Hof** (☑450 1000; www.mak.is). There
are loads of brochures, maps, internet access

and a great design shop. Knowledgable staff
can advise on tours and transport, including
walking tours of Akureyri. Website is extensive,
useful for planning.

Varmahlíð (p58)

Campsite   CAMPGROUND $
(☑899 3231; http://tjoldumiskagafirdi.is; sites per
person 1300kr, campsite tax 333kr; ⊙mid-May–mid-
Sep) Follow the signs from Hotel Varmahlíð
to reach this secluded, sheltered campground
above the town, near hiking trails.

★**Hestasport Cottages**   COTTAGE $$
(☑453 8383; www.riding.is/cottages; cottages
for 2/4/6 people 25,000/35,000/40,000kr; 🛜)
Perched on the hill above Varmahlíð, this
cluster of seven high-quality self-contained
timber cottages has good views, comfy rooms
and a very inviting stone hot-pot. Some sleep
six and all include kitchen facilities and
linen. They're excellent value, especially for
families and groups.

Alþýðulist   ARTS & CRAFTS
(☑453 7000; Rte 1; ⊙10am-6pm) In a sweet
turf-roofed house just next door to the
N1, this shop is crammed full of colourful
knitwear and handicrafts made in the Skagafjörður area. Look for the horse motif in
the *lopapeysur* (traditional Icelandic sweaters). The info centre is here too.

ⓘ Information

Tourist Information Centre (☑455 6161;
www.visitskagafjordur.is; Rte 1; ⊙9am-6pm
mid-May–Sep, 10am-4pm Mon-Fri rest of year;
🛜) In a turf house next to the service station,
shared with Alþýðulist gallery, this efficient
centre offers brochures and maps.

Hvammstangi (p59)

Kirkjuhvammur
Campsite
CAMPGROUND $

(☑899 0008; hvammur.camping@gmail.com; Kirk-juhvammi; sites per person 1200kr, campsite tax 333kr; ⊘early May–mid-Oct; ☞) The excellent, well-maintained Kirkjuhvammur campsite is up the hill near the photogenic old church. Find the turn-off near the town pool. The site has good facilities including a handy service building – with a large dining area where campers can eat – and there are nice walks in the area.

Mörk Homestay
GUESTHOUSE $$

(☑862 5466; Rte 711; d 25,000kr) Just north of town, this delightful waterfront property offers a modern, stylish fjordside cottage – your room's terrace is the perfect place to enjoy a cuppa and a water view. Breakfast (2500kr per person) is delivered to your room. Reserve on booking.com.

Hvammstangi
Cottages & Hostel
COTTAGE $$

(☑860 7700; www.stayinhvammstangi.is; Kirk-juhvammsvegur; cottages incl linen 18,200kr; ☞) A cluster of nine cookie-cutter cottages found by the campground. Each is petite but fully self-contained with bathroom, kitchenette and TV, and can sleep up to four (three beds, plus sofa bed) – although that would be snug. Their hostel is on the waterfront road (Norðurbraut 22a/Rte 711) and is a good deal with sleek rooms with shared baths and kitchen.

★Sjávarborg
ICELANDIC $$

(☑451 3131; www.sjavarborg-restaurant.is; Strand-gata 1; mains 2500-5000kr; ⊘11am-11pm, shorter hours Oct-May; ☞) Hats off to this stylish res-taurant above the Icelandic Seal Centre (p59). Reserve ahead for a table by vast picture win-dows offering fjord views and a menu that roves from seared tuna to gourmet burgers and slow-cooked lamb shank. The home-made blueberry ice cream is a treat (and more than big enough to share).

Borganes & Around (p62)

◎ Sights & Tours

Borgarfjörður Museum
MUSEUM

(Safnahús; ☑433 7200; www.safnahus.is; Bjar-narbraut 4-6; adult/child 1000kr/free; ⊘1-5pm May-Aug, 1-4pm Mon-Fri Sep-Apr) This small municipal museum has an engaging exhibit on the story of children in Iceland over the last 100 years. It's told through myriad pho-tographs and found items, and though it's accompanied by English translations, don't be shy about having museum staff show you through. The story behind each photograph is captivating; you'll be thinking about this exhibit long after you've left.

Oddsstaðir
HORSE RIDING

(☑435 1413; www.oddsstadir.is; Rte 512, Oddsstaðir farm) Multiday riding tours throughout West Iceland with a large team of horses.

★ᵏᵃ Festivals & Events

Brákarhátíð
CULTURAL

(www.brakarhatid.is; ⊘late Jun) A festival in hon-our of Þorgerður Brák, a heroine from *Egil's Saga*. Expect town decorations, parades, a concert and a lively, offshore, mud-football match.

🛏 Sleeping

Borgarnes HI Hostel
HOSTEL $

(☑695 3366; www.hostel.is; Borgarbraut 11-13; dm 5900kr, d with/without bathroom 18,200/16,300kr; @☞) This recently updated hostel has a sleek well-lit look in its public spaces, and clean, comfortable rooms. There's a 10% dis-count for HI members.

★Bjarg
GUESTHOUSE $$

(☑437 1925; www.facebook.com/bjargborgarnes; Bjarg farm; d with/without bathroom incl breakfast 20,700/17,300kr; ☞) One of the most beauti-fully situated places to stay in the area, this attractive series of linked cottages 1.5km north of Borgarnes overlooks the fjord and mountains. It has warm, cosy rooms with tasteful wood panelling and crisp white lin-ens. There are shared guest kitchens, a good buffet breakfast, a BBQ, spotless bathrooms, and a turf-roofed cottage that sleeps four.

Ensku Húsin
GUESTHOUSE $$

(☑437 1826; http://enskuhusin.is; Rte 54; d with/without bathroom incl breakfast 24,900/20,500kr; ☞) Located 8km northwest of central Bor-garnes off Rte 54, this former fishing lodge with a dramatic riverside setting has been refitted with generous amounts of old-school charm. Upstairs rooms retain much of the long-ago feel, and there's a newer block with additional rooms. The friendly owners also offer accommodation in a restored farm-house 2km away.

Fossatún HOTEL $$

(☑ 433 5800; www.fossatun.is; Rte 50; hut/cottage 8700/31,000kr, d with/without bathroom from 22,000/14,800kr; @ 🛜) This family-friendly spot has a guesthouse, hotel, full cottage and camping huts next to a beautiful roaring waterfall. The spacious on-site **restaurant** (mains 1600-3000kr) overlooks the falls and themed walking paths. It's on the southern branch of Rte 50, about 23km east of Borgarnes and 18km southwest of Reykholt. The friendly owner is a well-known children's book author (minigolf and a playground keep things kid-focused) and former record producer (there's an amazing 3000-record collection, *and* you can play 'em).

✖ Eating & Drinking

★ **Settlement Centre**
Restaurant INTERNATIONAL $$

(☑ 437 1600; www.landnam.is; Brákarbraut 13; lunch buffet 2200kr, mains 2200-4600kr; ⊘10am-9pm; 🛜) The Settlement Centre's restaurant, set in a light-filled room built into the rock face, is airy, upbeat and one of the region's best bets for food. Choose from traditional Icelandic and international eats (lamb, fish stew etc). The lunch buffet (11.30am to 3pm) is very popular. Book ahead for dinner. While you wait, flip to the back of the menu and read up on the history of the town's oldest buildings (including the one you're sitting in).

Steðji Brugghús BREWERY

(☑ 896 5001; www.stedji.com; tasting 1500kr; ⊘1-5pm Mon-Sat) This little family-run brewhouse 25km north of Borgarnes off Rte 50 has a good range of local beers, from strawberry beer to lager and seasonal beers. Try them in the microbrewery's tasting room.

🛍 Shopping

★ **Ljómalind** MARKET

(Farmers Market; ☑ 437 1400; www.ljomalind.is; Brúartorg 4; ⊘10am-6pm May-Sep, noon-5pm Oct-Apr) 🖉 A long-standing collaboration between local producers, this packed farmers market sits at the edge of town near the roundabout. It stocks everything from fresh dairy products from **Erpsstaðir** (☑ 868 0357; www.erpsstadir.is; Rte 60; cowshed tour adult/child 600kr/free; ⊘11am-6pm mid-Jun–mid-Aug, 1-5pm mid-May–mid-Jun & mid-Aug–mid-Sep; 👼) and organic meat to locally made bath products, handmade wool sweaters, jewellery and all manner of imaginative collectables.

ℹ Information

Tourist Information Centre (☑ 437 2214; www.west.is; Borgarbraut 58-60; ⊘9am-5pm Mon-Fri, 10am-4pm Sat, noon-4pm Sun Jun-Aug, 9am-5pm Mon-Fri Sep-May; 🛜) West Iceland's well-informed main tourist information centre; in the big shopping centre.

ROAD TRIP ESSENTIALS

Iceland Driving Guide

Driving in Iceland gives you unparalleled freedom to discover the country and, thanks to (relatively) good roads and (relatively) light traffic, it's all fairly straightforward.

DRIVING LICENCE & DOCUMENTS

You can drive in Iceland with a driving licence from the US, Canada, Australia, New Zealand and most European countries. If your licence is not in Roman script, you need an International Driving Permit (normally issued by your home country's automobile association).

If you're bringing your own car on the ferry, you'll also need the vehicle's registration documents and proof of valid insurance (a 'green card' if your car isn't registered in a Nordic or EU-member country).

INSURANCE

A vehicle registered in Nordic or EU-member countries is considered to have valid automobile insurance in Iceland. If your vehicle is registered in a non-Nordic or non-EU country, you'll need a 'green card',

which proves that you are insured to drive while in Iceland. Green cards are issued by insurance companies in your home country; contact your existing insurer.

When hiring a car, check the small print; most vehicles come with third-party insurance and CDW to cover you for damage to the car. Also check the excess (the initial amount you will be liable to pay in the event of an accident) as this can be surprisingly high.

Hire vehicles are not covered for damage to tyres, headlights and windscreens, or damage caused to the car's underside by driving on dirt roads, through water or in ash- or sandstorms. Many companies will try to sell you additional insurance to cover these possibilities. You need to consider whether this is appropriate for you and your plans, and how prepared you are to cough up in the event of such occurrences (and the cost of the insurance versus factors such as the length of your

Driving Tips

➡ Driving coastal areas can be spectacularly scenic, and incredibly slow as you weave up and down over mountain passes and in and out of long fjords.

➡ A 2WD vehicle will get you almost everywhere in summer (note: not into the highlands, or on F roads).

➡ In winter heavy snow can cause many roads to close; mountain roads generally only open in June and may start closing as early as September. For up-to-date information on road conditions, visit www.road.is.

➡ Don't be pressured into renting a GPS unit – if you purchase a good, up-to-date touring map, and can read it, you should be fine without GPS. If you are planning to take remote trails, it will be worthwhile.

Fast Facts: Driving

Right or left? Drive on the right

Manual or automatic? Most rental agencies offer both

Legal driving age 17 (20 or 21 for rentals)

Top Speed Limit 90km/h (rural paved roads)

Headlights On at all times

Signature Car High-clearance 4WD

rental and what regions you plan to visit). There is no way of predicting what climatic conditions you might meet on your trip.

MAPS

In recent years Iceland has been busy building new roads and tunnels, and sealing gravel stretches. We recommend you purchase a recently updated country map – ensure it shows the rerouted Ring Road (rerouted in East Iceland in late 2017).

Tourist information centres have useful free maps of their town and region. They also stock the free tourist booklet *Around Iceland,* which has info and town plans.

Tourist info centres, petrol stations and bookshops all sell road atlases and maps.

Map publisher Ferðakort (www.ferda kort.is) sells online and has a dedicated map department at Iðnú bookshop (☎517 7210; Brautarholt 8; ⏰10am-4pm Mon-Fri) in Reykjavík. Forlagið (Mál og Menning) is another reputable map publisher with a wide range; browse at its store in the capital or online (www.forlagid.is – click on 'landakort'). Both companies have good touring maps of Iceland (1:500,000 or 1:600,000; approximately kr2000), useful for general driving.

HIRING A CAR

Travelling by car is the only way to get to some parts of Iceland. Although car-hire rates are very expensive by international standards, they compare favourably to bus or internal air travel, especially if there are a few of you to split the costs. Shop around and book online for the best deals.

To rent a car you must be 20 years old (23 to 25 years for a 4WD) and hold a valid licence.

The cheapest cars, usually a small hatchback or similar, cost from around 8000kr per day in high season (June to August). Figure on paying around 10,000kr to 12,000kr for the smallest 4WD that offers higher clearance than a regular

F Roads

While the Ring Road is all drivable with a 2WD, most inland roads crossing stretches of the jagged highlands are designated 'F roads'. We can think of a few choice F words for these bumpy, at times almost-nonexistent tracts of land, but in reality the 'F' stands for *fjall* (mountain). Do not confuse F roads with gravel stretches of road (regular gravel roads are normally fine for 2WDs, although some of them are bumpy rides for small, low-clearance cars).

➡ F roads are indicated on maps and road signs with an 'F' preceding the road number (F26, F88 etc).

➡ Opening dates vary with weather conditions, but are generally around mid-to late June.

➡ F roads only support 4WDs. If you travel on F roads in a hired 2WD you'll in-validate your insurance. F roads are unsafe for small cars: do yourself a favour and steer clear, or hire a 4WD (or take a bus or super-Jeep tour).

➡ Before tackling any F road, educate yourself about what lies ahead (eg river crossings) and whether or not the entire route is open. See www.road.is for mountain-road opening details.

➡ While some F roads may almost blend into the surrounding nature, driving off marked tracks is strictly prohibited everywhere in Iceland, as it damages fragile ecosystems.

car but isn't advised for large river crossings, and 15,000kr to 20,000kr for a larger 4WD model.

Rates include unlimited mileage and VAT (a hefty 24%), and usually collision damage waiver (CDW). Weekly rates offer some discount. From September to May you should be able to find considerably better daily rates and deals.

Check the small print, as additional costs such as extra insurance, airport pick-up charges, and one-way rental fees can add up.

In winter you should opt for a larger, sturdier car for safety reasons, preferably with 4WD (ie absolutely *not* a compact 2WD).

In the height of summer many companies run out of rentals. Book ahead.

Many travel organisations (eg Hostelling International Iceland, Hey Iceland) offer package deals that include car hire.

Most companies are based in the Reykjavík and Keflavík areas, with city and airport offices. Larger companies have extra locations around the country (usually in Akureyri and Egilsstaðir). Ferry passengers arriving via Seyðisfjörður should contact car-hire agencies in nearby Egilsstaðir.

Car-hire companies:

Átak (www.atak.is)

Avis (www.avis.is)

Budget (www.budget.is)

Cars Iceland (www.carsiceland.com)

Cheap Jeep (www.cheapjeep.is)

Europcar (www.europcar.is) The biggest hire company in Iceland.

Geysir (www.geysir.is)

Go Iceland (www.goiceland.com)

Hertz (www.hertz.is)

SADcars (www.sadcars.com)

Saga (www.sagacarrental.is)

Car Sharing

There are a couple of peer-to-peer car-sharing platforms in Iceland, including Carrenters (www.carrenters.is). There are also locals' cars and campervans occasionally available for rent via airbnb.com.

These platforms offer people the chance to hire privately owned cars from locals. If you take up this option, do your homework and assess the costs and the small print – from our research, some prices were not much different from those of car-hire companies; cars were sometimes quite old; and you don't have the reassurance of a company behind you to help if things go wrong.

Road Trip Websites

Five websites every traveller should know about:

Carpooling in Iceland (www.samferda.is) Handy site that helps drivers and passengers link up. Passengers often foot some of the petrol bill. A savvy alternative to hitching (for passengers), and a way to help pay for car rental and fuel (for drivers).

Icelandic Met Office (www.vedur.is) Get a reliable forecast from this site (or call 902 0600, and press 1 after the introduction). Download its app, too (called Vedur).

Public Transport (www.public transport.is) An impressive map and searchable database of all public-transport services in the country.

Safetravel (www.safetravel.is) Learn about minimising risks while travelling in Iceland.

Vegagerðin (www.road.is) Iceland's road administration site details road openings and closings around the country. Vital for information about winter road access.

Motorcycles

Biking Viking (www.rmc.is/en/biking-viking) offers motorcycle rental, tours and service.

Campervans

Combining accommodation and transport costs into campervan rental is a booming option – and has extra appeal in summer, as it allows for some spontaneity (unlike every other form of accommodation, campsites don't need to be prebooked). Travelling by campervan in winter is possible, but we don't recommend it – there are fewer facilities open for campers at this time, and weather conditions may make it unsafe.

Large car-hire companies usually have campervans for rent, but there are also more offbeat choices, offering from backpacker-centric to family-sized, or real 4WD set-ups for highland exploration. Some companies offer gear rental to help your trip go smoothly (GPS, cooking gear and stove, barbecue, sleeping bags, camping chairs, fishing equipment, portable wi-fi hot spots etc).

There are dozens of companies that can help you get set up. As with rental cars, prices vary depending on size and age of the vehicle, length of rental period, high/low season, added extras etc. Shop around, and read the fine print. Prices for something small and basic can start at around 12,000kr per day.

Camp Easy (www.campeasy.com)

Camper Iceland (www.campericeland.is)

Go Campers (www.gocampers.is)

Happy Campers (www.happycampers.is)

JS Camper Rental (www.jscamper.com) Truck campers on 4WD pick-ups.

Rent Nordic (www.rent.is)

ROADS & CONDITIONS

Good main-road surfaces and light traffic (especially outside the capital and Southwest region) make driving in Iceland relatively easy, but there are some specific hazards. Watch the 'Drive Safely on Icelandic Roads' video on www.drive.is for more.

Livestock Sheep graze in the countryside over the summer, and often wander onto roads. Slow down when you see livestock on or near roadsides.

Unsurfaced roads The transition from sealed to gravel roads is marked with the warning sign 'Malbik Endar' – slow right down to avoid skidding when you hit the gravel. Most accidents involving foreign drivers in Iceland are caused by the use of excessive speed on unsurfaced roads. If your car does begin to skid, take your foot off the accelerator and gently turn the car in the direction you want the front wheels to go. Do not brake.

Blind rises In most cases, roads have two lanes with steeply cambered sides and no hard shoulder; be prepared for oncoming traffic in the centre of the road, and slow down and stay to the right when approaching a blind rise, marked as 'Blindhæð' on road signs.

Single-lane bridges Slow down and be prepared to give way when approaching single-lane bridges (marked as 'Einbreið Brú'). Right of way is with the car closest to the bridge.

Sun glare With the sun often sitting low to the horizon, sunglasses are recommended.

Winter conditions In winter make sure your car is fitted with winter tyres, and carry a shovel, blankets, food and water.

Ash- & sandstorms Volcanic ash and severe sandstorms can strip paint off cars; strong winds can even topple your vehicle. At-risk areas are marked with orange warning signs.

F roads (p108) Roads suitable for 4WD vehicles only.

River crossings Few highland roads have bridges over rivers. Fords are marked on maps with a 'V'.

Tunnels There are a number of tunnels in Iceland – a couple are single lane, and a little anxiety-inducing! Before you enter such tunnels, a sign will indicate which direction has right of way. There will be a couple of pull-over bays inside the tunnel (signed 'M'). If the passing bay is on your side in the tunnel, you are obligated to pull in and let oncoming traffic pass you.

ROAD RULES

➡ Drive on the right.

➡ Front and rear seatbelts are compulsory.

➡ Dipped headlights must be on at all times.

Driving Problem-Buster

What if my hire car breaks down? Your rental agency should provide you with an assistance number.

And my own car? You may have reciprocal cover with the Icelandic motoring association Félag Íslenskra Bifreiðaeigenda (FÍB; www.fib.is) – check with your home association. FÍB's 24-hour breakdown number is 511 2112. Even if you're not a member, it can provide info and numbers for towing and breakdown services.

What about winter? If you're driving in winter, carry food, water and blankets in your car. Hire cars are generally fitted with snow tyres.

Road Distances (km)

	Akureyri	Borgarnes	Egilsstaðir	Geysir	Höfn	Hvammstangi	Reykjahlíð	Reykjavík	Skaftafell	Skógar
Borgarnes	315									
Egilsstaðir	265	570								
Geysir	300	150	620							
Höfn	450	520	190	440						
Hvammstangi	200	120	460	270	640					
Reykjahlíð	100	410	170	390	355	295				
Reykjavík	390	70	640	100	450	190	470			
Skaftafell	410	385	310	305	130	505	455	320		
Skógar	520	215	480	135	300	335	625	150	170	
Vík	550	245	450	165	270	365	595	180	140	30

➡ Blood alcohol limit is 0.05%.

➡ Mobile phone use is prohibited when driving except with a hands-free kit.

➡ Children under six years must use a car seat.

➡ Do not drive off-road (ie off marked roads and 4WD trails).

Speed Limits

➡ Built-up areas: 50km/h

➡ Unsealed roads: 80km/h

➡ Sealed roads: 90km/h

FUEL

➡ Petrol stations are regularly spaced around the country, but in the highlands you should check fuel levels and the distance to the next station before setting off.

➡ At the time of research, unleaded petrol and diesel cost about kr225 (€1.60) per litre.

Buying Fuel

Most smaller petrol stations are unstaffed, and all pumps are automated. There is the (time-consuming) option of going inside a staffed service station to ask staff to switch the pump to manual, enabling you to fill up and pay for your fuel afterwards, but not all places offer such a service.

To fill up using the automated service:

➡ Put your credit card into the machine's slot (you'll need a card with a four-digit PIN) and follow the instructions.

➡ The next step is determined by the type of payment machine. On newer touchscreens you can press 'Full Tank', or you input the maximum amount you wish to spend, then wait while the pump authorises your purchase. Entering a maximum amount pre-approves your card for that capped amount, but you are only charged for the cost of the fuel put into your vehicle (this can be any amount you wish, up to the pre-approved capped amount).

➡ Select the pump number you are using.

➡ Fill tank.

➡ If you require a receipt, re-enter your card into the slot.

The first time you fill up, visit a staffed station while it's open, in case you have any problems. Note that you need a PIN for your card to use the automated pumps. If you don't have a PIN, buy prepaid cards from an N1 station that you can then use at the automated pumps.

Iceland Travel Guide

GETTING THERE & AWAY

Iceland has become far more accessible in recent years, with more flights arriving from more destinations. Ferry transport (from northern Denmark) makes a good alternative for Europeans wishing to take their own car.

Flights, cars and tours can be booked online at lonelyplanet.com/bookings.

AIR

Keflavík International Airport (KEF; ☑425 6000; www.kefairport.is; Reykjanesbraut; ☉24hr) Iceland's main international airport is 48km southwest of Reykjavík.

Reykjavík Domestic Airport (Reykjavíkurflugvöllur; Map p74; www.isavia.is; Innanlandsflug) Internal flights and those to Greenland and the Faroes use this small airport in central Reykjavík.

A growing number of airlines fly to Iceland (including budget carriers) from destinations in Europe and North America. Some airlines have services only from June to August. Find a list of airlines serving the country at www.visiticeland.com (under Plan Your Trip/Flights).

Eagle Air (☑562 2640; www.eagleair.is; Reykjavík Domestic Airport) Scheduled domestic flights to small airstrips.

Icelandair (www.icelandair.com) The national carrier has an excellent safety record.

WOW Air (www.wowair.com) Icelandic low-cost carrier, serving a growing number of European and North American destinations.

SEA

Smyril Line (www.smyrilline.com) operates a pricey but well-patronised weekly car ferry, the *Norröna,* from Hirtshals (Denmark) through Tórshavn (Faroe Islands) to Seyðisfjörður in East Iceland. It operates year-round, although winter passage is weather-dependent – see website for more.

Fares vary greatly, depending on dates of travel, what sort of vehicle (if any) you are travelling with, and cabin selection. Sailing time is around 36 hours from Denmark to the Faroe Islands, and 19 hours from the Faroes to Iceland.

It's possible to make a stopover in the Faroes. Contact Smyril Line or see the website for trip packages.

DIRECTORY A–Z

ACCESSIBLE TRAVEL

Iceland can be trickier than many places in northern Europe when it comes to access for travellers with disabilities.

For details on accessible facilities, contact the information centre for people with disabilities, **Þekkingarmiðstöð Sjálfsbjargar** (Sjálfsbjörg Knowledge Centre; Map p74; ☑550 0118; www.thekkingarmidstod.is; Hátún 12, Reykjavík).

A good resource is the website God Adgang (www.godadgang.dk), a Danish initiative adopted in Iceland. Follow the instructions to find Icelandic service providers that have been assessed for the accessibility label.

Particularly good for tailor-made accessible trips around the country are All Iceland Tours (http://alliceland.is) and Iceland Unlimited (www.icelandunlimited.is). Gray Line Iceland (www.grayline.is)

and Reykjavík Excursions (www.re.is) run sightseeing and day tours from Reykjavík and will assist travellers with special needs, but they recommend you contact them in advance to discuss your requirements.

Reykjavík's city buses are accessible courtesy of ramps; elsewhere, however, public buses don't have ramps or lifts.

Download Lonely Planet's free Accessible Travel guide from http://lptravel.to/AccessibleTravel.

Sleeping Price Ranges

The following price categories are based on the high-season price for a double room:

€ less than 15,000kr (€120)

€€ 15,000–30,000kr (€120–240)

€€€ more than 30,000kr (€240)

ACCOMMODATION

Iceland has a broad range of accommodation, but demand often outstrips supply. If you're visiting in the shoulder and high seasons (from May to September), book early.

Camping

Tjaldsvæði (organised campsites) are found in almost every town, at some rural farmhouses and along major hiking trails. The best sites have washing machines, cooking facilities and hot showers, but others just have a cold-water tap and a toilet block. Some are attached to the local *sundlaug* (swimming pool), with shower facilities provided by the pool for a small fee.

Icelandic weather is notoriously fickle, and if you intend to camp it's wise to invest in a good-quality tent. There are a few outfits in Reykjavík that offer rental of camping equipment, and some car-hire companies can also supply you with gear such as tents, sleeping mats and cooking equipment.

With the increase in visitors to Iceland, campgrounds are getting busier, and service blocks typically housing two toilets and one shower are totally insufficient for coping with the demand of dozens of campers. If the wait is long, consider heading to the local swimming pool and paying to use the amenities there.

It is rarely necessary (or possible) to book a camping spot in advance. Many small-town campsites are unstaffed – look for a contact number for the caretaker posted on the service block, or an instruction to head to the tourist information centre or swimming pool to pay; alternatively, a caretaker may visit the campsite in the evening to collect fees.

A few things to keep in mind:

➡ When camping in parks and reserves the usual rules apply: leave sites as you find them; use biodegradable soaps; and carry out your rubbish.

➡ Campfires are not allowed, so bring a stove. Butane cartridges and petroleum fuels are available in petrol stations. Blue Campingaz cartridges are not always readily available; the grey Coleman cartridges are more common.

➡ Camping with a tent or campervan/caravan usually costs 1200kr to 1900kr per person.

Practicalities

Weights and measures The metric system is used.

Discount cards Students and seniors qualify for discounts on internal flights, some ferry and bus fares, tours and museum entry fees. You'll need to show proof of student status or age. The Reykjavík City Card (p86) is useful in the capital.

DVDs Iceland falls within DVD zone 2.

Reykjavík Grapevine (www.grapevine.is) Excellent tourist-oriented and daily-life articles about Iceland, plus what's-on listings. Paper copy widely available and free.

Smoking Illegal in enclosed public spaces, including in cafes, bars, clubs, restaurants and on public transport. Most accommodation is nonsmoking.

Sleeping-Bag Accommodation

Iceland's best-kept secret is the sleeping-bag option offered by hostels, numerous guesthouses and some hotels. For a fraction of the normal cost, you'll get a bed without a duvet; you supply your own sleeping bag.

Taking the sleeping-bag option doesn't mean sleeping in a dorm – generally you book the same private room, just minus the linen. The sleeping-bag option usually means BYO towel, too, and it's also worth packing a pillowcase.

Sleeping-bag prices never include breakfast, but you'll often have the option to purchase it.

Note that the option to use your own sleeping bag is more prevalent outside the peak summer period.

Electricity is often an additional 800kr. Many campsites charge for showers.

➡ There's a 'lodging tax' of 333kr per site; some places absorb this cost in the per-person rate, others make you pay it in addition to the per-person rate.

➡ Consider purchasing the good-value Camping Card (www.campingcard.is), which costs €149 and covers 28 nights of camping at 41 campsites throughout the country for two adults and up to four children from mid-May to mid-September. Note that the card doesn't include the lodging tax, or any charges for electricity or showers. Full details online.

➡ Most campsites open mid-May to mid-September. Large campsites that also offer huts or cottages may be open year-round. This is a fluid situation, as an increasing number of visitors are hiring campervans in the cooler months and looking to camp with facilities – ask at local tourist offices for info and advice.

➡ If camping in summer, be aware that if the weather turns bad and you'd like to sleep with a roof over your head, you'll be extremely lucky to find last-minute availability in guesthouses or hostels.

➡ Free accommodation directory *Áning* (available from tourist information centres) lists many of Iceland's campsites, but is not exhaustive.

Farmhouse Accommodation

Many rural farmhouses offer campsites, sleeping-bag spaces, made-up guestrooms, and cabins and cottages. Over time, some 'farmhouses' have evolved into large country hotels.

Facilities vary: some farms provide meals or have a guest kitchen, some have outdoor hot-pots (hot tubs), and many provide horse riding or can organise activities such as fishing. Roadside signs signal which farmhouses provide accommodation and what facilities they offer.

Rates are similar to guesthouses in towns, with sleeping-bag accommodation around 7500kr and made-up beds from 11,000kr to 18,000kr per person. Breakfast is usually included in the made-up room price, while an evening meal (generally served at a set time) costs around 7000kr.

Guesthouses

The Icelandic term *gistiheimilið* (guesthouse) covers a broad range of properties, from family homes renting out a few rooms, to a cluster of self-contained cottages, to custom-built blocks of guestrooms.

Guesthouses vary enormously in character, from stylish, contemporary options to those with plain, chintzy or dated decor. A surprisingly high number only have rooms with shared bathroom.

Most are comfortable and cosy, with guest kitchens, TV lounges and buffet-style breakfasts (either included in the price or for around 2200kr extra). If access to a self-catering kitchen is important to you, it pays to ask beforehand to ensure availability.

Some guesthouses offer sleeping-bag accommodation at a price significantly reduced from that of a made-up bed. Many places don't advertise a sleeping-bag option, so it pays to ask.

As a general guide, sleeping-bag accommodation costs 7500kr per night, double rooms in summer 17,000kr to 26,000kr, and self-contained units excluding linen from 19,000kr. Guesthouse rooms with their own bathroom are often similarly priced to hotel rooms.

Hostels

Iceland has 34 well-maintained hostels administered by Hostelling International Iceland (www.hostel.is). In Reykjavík, Akureyri and a handful of other places, there are also independent backpacker hostels. Bookings are recommended at all of them, especially from June to August.

About half the HI hostels open year-round. Check online for opening-date info.

All hostels offer hot showers, cooking facilities and sleeping-bag accommodation, and most offer private rooms (some with private bathroom). Most prices now include linen, but if they don't, the price to hire linen is around 2000kr per person per stay.

Breakfast (where available) costs 1700kr to 2300kr.

Join Hostelling International (www.hihostels.com) in your home country to benefit from HI member discounts of 10% per person. Nonmembers pay from about 3800kr to 6500kr for a dorm bed with linen; single rooms start at 7500kr, and double rooms range from 10,000kr to 18,000kr (more for private bathrooms). Children aged four to 12 get a discount of 1500kr.

Hotels

Every major town has at least one business-style hotel, usually featuring comfortable but innocuous rooms with private bathroom, phone, TV and sometimes a minibar. Invariably hotels also have decent restaurants.

Summer prices for singles/doubles start at around 20,000/28,000kr and usually include a buffet breakfast. Rates for a double room at a nice but non-luxurious hotel in a popular tourist area in peak summer can easily top 34,000kr. Reykjavík high-end hotels and luxury country lodges top 50,000kr.

Prices drop substantially outside high season (June to August), and cheaper rates may be found online.

The largest local chains are Icelandair Hotels (www.icelandairhotels.is), Íslandshotel (www.islandshotel.is), which includes the brand Fosshótel, Keahotels (www.keahotels.is) and CenterHotels (www.centerhotels.is).

Many international hotel chains are opening in the growing Reykjavík market – Hilton recently added to its portfolio in the capital, and a new Marriott five-star Reykjavík Edition opened in late 2021.

ELECTRICITY

230V/50Hz

230V/50Hz

FOOD

If people know anything about Icelandic food, it's usually to do with a plucky population tucking into boundary-pushing dishes such as fermented shark or sheep's head. It's a pity the spotlight doesn't shine as brightly on Iceland's delicious, fresh-from-the-farm ingredients, the seafood

Eating Price Ranges

The following price ranges refer to a main course.

€ Less than 2000kr (€16)

€€ 2000–5000kr (€16–40)

€€€ More than 5000kr (€40)

bounty hauled from the surrounding icy waters, the innovative dairy products (hello, *skyr!*) or the clever, historic food-preserving techniques that are finding new favour with today's much-feted New Nordic chefs. Reykjavík, especially, has a burgeoning, creative food scene.

LGBTIQ+ TRAVELLERS

Icelanders have a very open, accepting attitude towards homosexuality, though the gay scene is quite low-key, even in Reykjavík (p85).

INTERNET ACCESS

Wi-fi is common in Iceland.

➜ Most accommodation and eating venues across the country offer wi-fi, and often buses do, too. Access is usually free for guests/customers. You may need to ask staff for an access code.

➜ Most of the N1 service stations have free wi-fi.

➜ The easiest way to get online is to buy an Icelandic SIM card with a data package and pop it in your unlocked smartphone. Other devices can then access the internet via the phone.

➜ To travel with your own wi-fi hot spot, check out Trawire (http://iceland.trawire.com) for portable 4G modem rental with unlimited usage from US$9 per day (up to 10 laptops or mobile devices can be connected).

➜ Some car- and campervan-hire companies offer portable modem devices as an optional extra.

➜ Most Icelandic libraries have computer terminals for public internet access, even in small towns; there's often a small fee.

➜ Tourist information centres often have public internet terminals, often free for brief usage.

MONEY

Iceland is an almost cashless society where credit cards reign supreme, even in the most rural reaches. PIN required for purchases. ATMs available in all towns.

ATMs

➜ As long as you're carrying a valid card, you'll need to withdraw only a limited amount of cash from ATMs.

➜ Almost every town in Iceland has a bank with an ATM (*hraðbanki*), where you can withdraw cash using MasterCard, Visa, Maestro or Cirrus cards.

➜ Diners Club and JCB cards connected to the Cirrus network have access to all ATMs.

➜ You'll also find ATMs at larger petrol stations and in shopping centres.

Credit & Debit Cards

➜ Locals use plastic for even small purchases.

➜ Contact your financial institution to make sure that your card is approved for overseas use – you will need a PIN for purchases.

➜ Visa and MasterCard are accepted in most shops, restaurants and hotels. Amex is usually accepted, Diners Club less so.

➜ You can pay for the Flybus from Keflavík International Airport to Reykjavík using plastic – handy if you've just arrived in the country.

➜ If you intend to stay in rural farmhouse accommodation or visit isolated villages, it's a good idea to carry enough cash to tide you over.

Currency

The Icelandic unit of currency is the króna (plural krónur), written as kr or ISK.

➜ Coins come in denominations of 1kr, 5kr, 10kr, 50kr and 100kr.

➜ Notes come in denominations of 500kr, 1000kr, 2000kr, 5000kr and 10,000kr.

➜ Some accommodation providers and tour operators quote their prices in euro to ward against currency fluctuations, but these must be paid in Icelandic currency.

Tipping

As service and VAT taxes are always included in prices, tipping isn't required in Iceland. Rounding up the bill at restaurants or leaving a small tip for good service is appreciated.

OPENING HOURS

Opening hours vary throughout the year (some places are closed outside the high season). In general hours tend to be longer from June to August, and shorter from September to May. Standard opening hours include the following:

Banks 9am–4pm Monday to Friday

Cafe-bars 10am–1am Sunday to Thursday, 10am to between 3am and 6am Friday and Saturday

Cafes 10am–6pm

Offices 9am–5pm Monday to Friday

Petrol stations 8am–10pm or 11pm (automated pumps open 24 hours)

Post offices 9am–4pm or 4.30pm Monday to Friday (to 6pm in larger towns)

Restaurants 11.30am–2.30pm and 6–9pm or 10pm

Shops 10am–6pm Monday to Friday, 10am–4pm Saturday; some Sunday opening in Reykjavík malls and major shopping strips

Supermarkets 9am–9pm

Vínbúðin (government-run liquor stores) Variable; many outside Reykjavík only open for a couple of hours per day

PUBLIC HOLIDAYS

Icelandic public holidays are usually an excuse for a family gathering or, when they occur on weekends, a reason to head to the countryside and go camping. If you're planning to travel during holiday periods, particularly the Commerce Day long weekend, you should book mountain huts and transport well in advance.

National public holidays in Iceland:

New Year's Day 1 January

Easter March or April; Maundy Thursday and Good Friday to Easter Monday (changes annually)

First Day of Summer First Thursday after 18 April

Labour Day 1 May

Ascension Day May or June (changes annually)

Whit Sunday and Whit Monday May or June (changes annually)

National Day 17 June

Commerce Day First Monday in August

Christmas 24 to 26 December

New Year's Eve 31 December

Changing Opening Hours

Some regional attractions and tourist-oriented businesses in Iceland are only open for a short summer season, typically from June to August. Reykjavík attractions and businesses generally run year-round.

As tourism is growing at a rapid pace, some regional businesses are vague about opening and closing dates; increasingly, seasonal restaurants or guesthouses may open sometime in May, or even April, and stay open until the end of September or into October if demand warrants it.

With the growth of winter tourism, an increasing number of businesses (especially on the Ring Road) are feeling their way towards year-round trading. Note that many Icelandic hotels and guesthouses close from Christmas Eve to New Year's Day.

Check websites and/or Facebook pages of businesses, and ask around for advice.

Note that many museums outside the capital only have regular, listed opening hours during summer (June to August). From September to May they may advertise restricted opening hours (eg a couple of hours once a week), but many places are happy to open for individuals on request, with a little forewarning – make contact via museum websites or local tourist offices.

SAFE TRAVEL

Iceland has a very low crime rate and in general any risks you'll face while travelling here are related to road safety, the unpredictable weather and the unique geological conditions.

A good place to learn about minimising your risks is Safetravel (www.safetravel.is). The website is an initiative of the Icelandic Association for Search and Rescue (ICE-SAR). The website also provides information on ICE-SAR's 112 Iceland app for smartphones (useful in emergencies), and explains procedures for leaving a travel plan with ICE-SAR or a friend/contact.

Geological Risks

➡ When hiking, river crossings can be dangerous, with glacial run-off transforming trickling streams into raging torrents on warm summer days.

➡ High winds can create vicious sandstorms in areas where there is loose volcanic sand.

➡ Hiking paths in coastal areas may only be accessible at low tide; seek local advice and obtain the relevant tide tables.

➡ In geothermal areas, stick to boardwalks or obviously solid ground. Avoid thin crusts of lighter-coloured soil around steaming fissures and mudpots.

➡ Be careful of the water in hot springs and mudpots – it often emerges from the ground at 100°C.

➡ In glacial areas beware of dangerous quicksand at the ends of glaciers, and never venture out onto the ice without crampons and ice axes (even then, watch out for crevasses).

➡ Snowfields may overlie fissures, sharp lava chunks or slippery slopes of scoria (volcanic slag).

➡ Always get local advice before hiking around live volcanoes.

➡ Only attempt isolated hiking and glacier ascents if you know what you're doing. Talk to locals and/or employ a guide.

Sustainable Travel

It can't be stressed enough: the fast and furious boom in tourism to Iceland is placing enormous pressure on the local population, the fragile environment, and the still-growing infrastructure. Your actions have consequences, so please endeavour to travel safely and tread lightly. Here are a few tips on staying safe and eco-aware (and on the good side of locals):

Heed local warnings and advice No one is trying to spoil your holiday – when a local tells you that your car isn't suitable for a particular road, or an area is off limits due to fear of a glacial outburst flood, it's because they know this country and what it's capable of. Be flexible, and change your plans when necessary.

Recognise your impact The numbers speak for themselves: 350,000 locals versus 2.2 million tourists in 2017. You may think that staying overnight in your campervan by a roadside isn't a problem. But it is when thousands of people do it – that's why there are laws banning it.

Plan properly Check weather-forecast and road-condition websites. Pack a good map, the appropriate gear, common sense and a degree of flexibility. No hiking in jeans, no attempting to cross rivers in small cars, no striding out onto glaciers without proper guidance and equipment.

Respect nature Subglacial volcanoes, geothermal areas and vast lava fields are big draws. That's why you're visiting Iceland, no? So take care not to damage them. If you've hired a 4WD, whatever you do, stick to marked roads; off-roading is illegal and causes irreparable damage to the fragile landscape.

Travel green Check out www.nature.is – it's chock-full of amazing tips on travelling sustainably in Iceland, and has an online map and apps with a goal of making ecofriendly choices easier for everyone.

→ It's rare to find warning signs or fences in areas where accidents can occur, such as large waterfalls, glacier fronts, cliff edges, and beaches with large waves and strong currents. Use common sense, and supervise children well.

TELEPHONE

→ Public payphones are extremely elusive in Iceland, but you may find them outside larger bus stations and petrol stations. Many accept credit cards as well as coins.

→ To make international calls from Iceland, first dial the international access code 00, then the country code, the area or city code, and the telephone number.

→ To phone Iceland from abroad, dial your country's international access code, Iceland's country code (354) and then the seven-digit phone number.

→ Iceland has no area codes.

→ Toll-free numbers begin with 800; mobile (cell) numbers start with 6, 7 or 8.

→ The online version of the phone book with good maps is at http://en.ja.is.

→ Useful numbers: directory enquiries 118 (local), 1811 (international).

Mobile Phones

Mobile (cell) coverage is widespread. Visitors with GSM phones can make roaming calls; purchasing a local SIM card with data package is the cheapest option if you're staying a while.

Emergency Numbers

For police, ambulance, fire and rescue services in Iceland, dial 112.

TOURIST INFORMATION

Websites

Official tourism sites for the country:

Inspired by Iceland (www.inspiredbyiceland.com)

Visit Iceland (www.visiticeland.com)

Each region also has its own useful site/s:

East Iceland (www.east.is)

North Iceland (www.northiceland.is; www.visitakureyri.is)

Reykjavík (www.visitreykjavik.is)

Southeast Iceland (www.south.is; www.visitvatnajokull.is)

Southwest Iceland (www.visitreykjanes.is; www.south.is)

West Iceland (www.west.is)

Westfjords (www.westfjords.is)

Smartphone Apps

Useful and practical smartphone apps include the vital 112 Iceland app for safe travel, Veður (weather), and apps for bus companies such as **Strætó** (☑540 2700; www.bus.is) and **Reykjavík Excursions** (Map p74; ☑580 5400; www.ioyo.is). Offline maps come in handy.

There are plenty more apps that cover all sorts of interests, from history and language to aurora-spotting, or walking tours of the capital. Reykjavík Grapevine's apps (Appy Hour, Craving and Appening) deserve special mention for getting you to the good stuff in the capital.

VISAS

Iceland is one of 26 member countries of the Schengen Convention, under which the EU countries (all but Bulgaria, Croatia, Romania, Cyprus, Ireland and the UK) plus Iceland, Norway, Liechtenstein and Switzerland have abolished checks at common borders.

The visa situation for Iceland is as follows:

→ Citizens of EU and Schengen countries – no visa required for stays of up to 90 days.

→ Citizens or residents of Australia, Canada, Japan, New Zealand, the UK and the USA – no visa required for tourist visits of up to 90 days.

→ Note that the total stay within the Schengen area must not exceed 90 days in any 180-day period.

→ Other countries – check online at www.utl.is.

Language

Icelandic belongs to the Germanic language family. It's related to Old Norse, and retains the letters 'eth' (ð) and 'thorn' (þ), which also existed in Old English. Be aware, especially when you're trying to read bus timetables or road signs, that place names can be spelled in several different ways due to Icelandic grammar rules. Most Icelanders speak English, but any attempts to speak the local language will be appreciated. If you read our pronunciation guides as if they were English, you'll be understood.

BASICS

Hello.	Halló.	ha·loh
Good morning.	Góðan daginn.	gohth-ahn dai-in
Goodbye.	Bless.	bles
Thank you.	Takk./Takk fyrir.	tak/ tak fi ·rir
Excuse me.	Afsakið.	af·sa·kidh
Sorry.	Fyrirgefðu.	fi ·rir·gev·dhu
Yes.	Já.	yow
No.	Nei.	nay

How are you?
Hvað segir þú gott? — kvadh se·yir thoo got

Fine. And you?
Allt fínt. En þú? — alt feent en thoo

Do you speak English?
Talar þú ensku? — ta·lar thoo ens·ku

I don't understand.
Ég skil ekki. — yekh skil e·ki

What's your name?
Hvað heitir þú? — kvadh hay·tir thoo

My name is ...
Ég heiti ... — yekh hay·ti ...

Signs

Inngangur	Entrance
Útgangur	Exit
Opið	Open
Lokað	Closed
Bannað	Prohibited
Snyrting	Toilets

DIRECTIONS

Where's the (hotel)?
Hvar er (hótelið)? — kvar er (hoh·te·lidh)

Can you show me (on the map)?
Geturðu sýnt mér (á kortinu)? — ge·tur·dhu seent myer (ow kor·ti·nu)

What's your address?
Hvert er heimilisfangið þitt? — kvert er hay·mi·lis·fan·gidh thit

EATING & DRINKING

What would you recommend?
Hverju mælir þú með? — kver·yu mai·lir thoo medh

Do you have vegetarian food?
Hafi ð þið grænmetisrétti? — ha·vidh thidh grain·me·tis·rye·ti

I'll have a ...
Ég ætla að fá ... — yekh ait·la adh fow ...

Cheers!
Skál! — skowl

I'd like a/the ..., please.
Get ég fengið ..., takk. — get yekh fen·gidh ... tak

table for (four)	borð fyrir (fjóra)	bordh fi·rir (fyoh·ra)
bill	reikninginn	rayk·nin·gin
drink list	vínseðillinn	veen·se·dhit·lin
menu	matseðillinn	mat·se·dhit·lin
that dish	þennan rétt	the·nan ryet
bottle of beer	bjór flösku	byohr·fleus ku
cup of coffee/tea	kaffi /te bolla	ka fi /te bot·la

glass of wine	*vín glas*	*veen* glas
water	*vatn*	vat
breakfast	*morgunmat*	*mor·gun·mat*
lunch	*hádegismat*	*how·de·yis·mat*
dinner	*kvöldmat*	*kveuld·mat*

EMERGENCIES

Help!	*Hjálp!*	hyowlp
Go away!	*Farðu!*	*far·dhu*
Call ...!	*Hringdu á ...!*	*hring·du ow ...!*
a doctor	*lækni*	*laik·ni*
the police	*lögregluna*	*leu·rekh·lu·na*

I'm lost.
Ég er villtur/villt. (m/f)   yekh er *vil·*tur/vilt

Where are the toilets?
Hvar er snyrtingin?   kvar er *snir·*tin·gin

SHOPPING & SERVICES

i'm looking for ...
Ég leita að ...   yekh *lay·*ta adh ...

How much is it?
Hvað kostar þetta?   kvadh kos·tar the·ta

That's too expensive.
Þetta er of dýrt.   the·ta er of deert

It's faulty.
Það er gallað.   thadh er *gat·*ladh

Where's the ...?
Hvar er ...?   kvar er ...

bank	*bankinn*	*bown·kin*
market	*markaðurinn*	*mar·ka·dhu·rin*
post office	*pósthúsið*	*pohst·hoo·sidh*

TRANSPORT

Can we get there by public transport?
Er hægt að taka   er haikht adh *ta·*ka
rútu þangað?   roo·tu *thown·*gadh

Where can I buy a ticket?
Hvar kaupi ég miða?   kvar *köy·*pi yekh *mi·*dha

Is this the ...	*Er þetta ...*	er *the·*ta ...
to (Akureyri)?	*til (Akureyrar)?*	til (*a·*ku·ray·rar)
boat	*ferjan*	*fer·*yan
bus	*rútan*	*roo·*tan
plane	*flugvélin*	*flukh·*vye·lin

Numbers

1	*einn*	aydn
2	*tveir*	tvayr
3	*þrír*	threer
4	*fjórir*	*fyoh·*rir
5	*fimm*	fim
6	*sex*	seks
7	*sjö*	syeu
8	*átta*	*ow·*ta
9	*níu*	*nee·*u
10	*tíu*	*tee·*u
20	*tuttugu*	*tu·*tu·gu
30	*þrjátíu*	*throw·*tee·u
40	*fjörutíu*	*fyeur·*tee·u
50	*fimmtíu*	*fim·*tee·u
60	*sextíu*	*seks·*tee·u
70	*sjötíu*	*syeu·*tee·u
80	*áttatíu*	*ow·*ta·tee·u
90	*níutíu*	*nee·*tee·u
100	*hundrað*	*hun·*dradh

What time's the ... bus?	*Hvenær fer ... strætisvagninn?*	*kve·*nair fer ... *strai·*tis·vag·nin
first	*fyrsti*	*firs·*ti
last	*síðasti*	*see·*dhas·ti
One ... ticket (to Reykjavík), please.	*Einn miða ... (til Reykjavíkur), takk.*	aitn *mi·*dha ... (til *rayk·*ya·vee·kur) tak
one-way	*aðra leiðina*	*adh·*ra *lay·*dhi·na
return	*fram og til baka*	fram okh til *ba·*ka
I'd like a taxi ...	*Get ég fengið leigubíl ...*	get yekh *fen·*gidh *lay·*gu·beel ...
at (9am)	*klukkan (níu fyrir hádegi)*	*klu·*kan (*nee·*u *fi·*rir *how·*de·yi)
tomorrow	*á morgun*	ow *mor·*gun

How much is it to ...?
Hvað kostar til ... ?   kvadh *kos·*tar til ...

Please stop here.
Stoppaðu hér, takk.   *sto·*pa·dhu hyer tak

Please take me to (this address).
Viltu aka mér til   *vil·*tu *a·*ka myer til
(þessa staðar)?   (the·sa sta·dhar)

BEHIND THE SCENES

SEND US YOUR FEEDBACK

We love to hear from travellers – your comments help make our books better. We read every word, and we guarantee that your feedback goes straight to the authors. Visit **lonelyplanet. com/contact** to submit your updates and suggestions.

Note: We may edit, reproduce and incorporate your comments in Lonely Planet products such as guidebooks, websites and digital products, so let us know if you don't want your comments reproduced or your name acknowledged. For a copy of our privacy policy visit lonelyplanet.com/privacy.

WRITER THANKS

ALEXIS AVERBUCK

Life in Iceland wouldn't be the same without the brilliant support of Carolyn Bain. She shared her friends and her ace tips on this great land with utmost generosity. Folks such as Halldór at Visit North Iceland and Addi, Anton, Stefán, Jóhanna, Finnur, Villi, Elisabet and Odinn and others I met along the way graciously shared their stories and their ideas. Thanks, too, to my own personal peachy King of the Mountains, RVB.

CAROLYN BAIN

Heartfelt thanks go to Icelandic friends, old and new, for making my relocation to Reykjavík such a rewarding move. As ever, a huge cast of locals, travellers and expats helped make this research project a delight, and I'm grateful to all of them for helping me see more, understand more and enjoy more. Cheers to Clifton Wilkinson

for the job, and bouquets to my co-authors for their collaborative spirit, especially to Alexis and Belinda for sparking gin-soaked dreams of future projects.

JADE BREMNER

Thanks to Clifton Wilkinson for his superb destination and publishing knowledge, plus everyone behind the scenes on this project – Cheree Broughton, Dianne, Jane, Neill Coen, Evan Godt and Helen Elfer. Last but not least, thanks to my travelling accomplice Harriet Sinclair, who joined me for a few epic days scaling Hekla volcano and walking the legendary Fimmvorduhals trail.

BELINDA DIXON

What an extraordinary opportunity – to drive pitted roads beside vast fjords, soaking in hot-pots along the way. Thanks as big as those mountains go to the whole Lonely Planet team and all who've shared

information and inspiration, including Magnus in Djúpavík, Charis in Reykjanes, Kári and Thomas in Ísafjörður and Eyþor in Flateyri. And to the warmest, wisest collaborators a writer could wish for: Alexis Averbuck and Carolyn Bain – raising a snúður to you both!

ACKNOWLEDGEMENTS

Climate map data adapted from Peel MC, Finlayson BL & McMahon TA (2007) 'Updated World Map of the Köppen-Geiger Climate Classification', Hydrology and Earth System Sciences, 11, 163344.

Front cover photograph: Mountains seen from the Ring Road, Shane WP Wongperk/ Shutterstock ©

Back cover photograph: Ice rocks on Jökulsárlón beach, b-hide the scene/Shutterstock ©

THIS BOOK

This 3rd edition of Lonely Planet's *Iceland's Ring Road* guidebook was researched and written by Alexis Averbuck, Carolyn Bain, Jade Bremner, Belinda Dixon. The previous two editions were written by Alexis, Carolyn, Jade, Belinda and Andy Symington. This guidebook was produced by the following:

Destination Editor
Clifton Wilkinson

Commissioning Editors
Genna Patterson, Daniel Bolger

Senior Cartographer
Valentina Kremenchutskaya

Cartographer Hunor Csutoros

Product Editors Kate James, James Appleton

Book Designers Fergal Condon, Virginia Moreno

Assisting Editors
Judith Bamber, Imogen Bannister, Victoria Harrison, Gabrielle Innes, Kate Morgan, Monique Perrin

Cover Researcher Naomi Parker

Thanks to Grace Dobell, Mateusz Kmiecinski, Darren O'Connell, Joe Piscotty, Amanda Williamson

INDEX

000 Map pages

000 Map pages

OUR WRITERS

ALEXIS AVERBUCK

Alexis has travelled and lived all over the world, from Sri Lanka to Ecuador, Zanzibar and Antarctica. In recent years she's been living on the Greek island of Hydra; sampling oysters in Brittany and careening through hill-top villages in Provence; and adventuring along Iceland's lava fields, sparkling fjords and glacier tongues. A travel writer for more than two decades, Alexis is also a painter – visit www.alexisaverbuck.com.

CAROLYN BAIN

A travel writer and editor for more than 20 years, Carolyn has lived, worked and studied in various corners of the globe, including Denmark, London, St Petersburg and Nantucket. She has authored more than 50 Lonely Planet titles, with her all-time favourite research destination being Iceland. Her love of the country recently led her to relocate from Melbourne, Australia to Reykjavík.

JADE BREMNER

Jade has been a journalist for more than a decade. She has lived in and reported on four different regions. Wherever she goes she finds action sports to try, the weirder the better, and it's no coincidence that many of her favourite places have some of the best waves in the world. Jade has edited travel magazines and sections for *Time Out* and *Radio Times* and has contributed to the *Times*, CNN and the *Independent*.

BELINDA DIXON

Only happy when her feet are suitably sandy, Belinda has been (gleefully) travelling, researching and writing for Lonely Planet since 2006. It's seen her navigating mountain passes and soaking in hot pots in Iceland's Westfjords, gazing at Verona's frescoes and fossil hunting on Dorset's Jurassic Coast. Belinda is also a podcaster and adventure writer and helps lead wilderness expeditions; see belindadixon.com.

Published by Lonely Planet Global Limited
CRN 554153
3rd edition – April 2022
ISBN 978 1 78868 080 6
© Lonely Planet 2022   Photographs © as indicated 2022
10 9 8 7 6 5 4 3 2 1
Printed in China

Although the authors and Lonely Planet have taken all reasonable care in preparing this book, we make no warranty about the accuracy or completeness of its content and, to the maximum extent permitted, disclaim all liability arising from its use.